Sustainability and the City

Sustainability and the City

The Service Approach

Adi Wolfson

BEP BUSINESS EXPERT PRESS

Sustainability and the City: The Service Approach

First published in 2018 by
Business Expert Press, LLC
222 East 46th Street, New York, NY 10017
www.businessexpertpress.com

ISBN-13: 978-1-94744-191-0 (paperback)
ISBN-13: 978-1-94744-192-7 (e-book)

Business Expert Press Service Systems and Innovations in Business and Society Collection

Collection ISSN: 2326-2664 (print)
Collection ISSN: 2326-2699 (electronic)

Cover and interior design by Exeter Premedia Services Private Ltd., Chennai, India

First edition: 2018

10 9 8 7 6 5 4 3 2 1

Printed in the United States of America.

Abstract

Cities are without a doubt one of the miracles of human creation and the embodiment of the human environment. Insofar as they are large and densely populated human settlements with defined legal and political boundaries that comprise clusters of buildings, open spaces, public facilities, and infrastructure, cities are mainly spaces of services that are exchanged between a wide variety of stakeholders, namely, residents, traders, visitors, and the city authorities. Moreover, the provision of cities' services has profound effect on the local and global sustainability. Thus, municipal services should comprise environmental, social, and economic values, which are designed, produced, and delivered in concert.

Over the years, a variety of new urban models and concepts have been designed and proposed as viable means to reestablish the bond between the human and the natural environments, to increase the quality of life within cities and to reduce the impacts that cities have on the social and natural environments (e.g., sustainable city, smart city, or resilient city). Herein, a new model of the service city is presented, including architecture and several pertinent examples, which considers it as a platform that manages and integrates the services and systems currently provided by the city while offering additional supporting services to increase the effectiveness of the value and to achieve the goal of sustainability.

Keywords

city, municipal services, service, smart city, sustainability

Contents

Quotes

Who am I

Who am I to speak
on behalf of the trees and for the
stones, to be a mouth for the wind and water,
to become a voice crying in the wilderness
for the winged creatures and quadrupeds,
to prophesy.
I. One. Tiny.
I who memorize day after day my dimensions
who seek my place
In the un-limited universe who
I

by Adi Wolfson
translated by Michael R. Burch

Preface

Cities are without a doubt one of the miracles of human creation and the embodiment of the human environment. As such, cities—the manifestation of human imagination and skills—comprise synthetic materials and artificial technologies and provide human services. Insofar as they are large and densely populated human settlements with defined legal and political boundaries that comprise clusters of buildings, open spaces, public facilities, and infrastructure, cities are mainly spaces of services that are exchanged between a wide variety of stakeholders—namely, residents, traders, visitors, and the city authorities. In addition, as today more than 50 percent of the world's population lives in urban areas, a proportion that will grow tremendously in the coming decades, and as most economic and social activities are performed in cities, the effect of cities' services on sustainability as practiced by their residents as well as by the whole world should be studied and designed. Moreover, municipal services should comprise environmental, social, and economic values, which are designed, produced, and delivered in concert by the municipal authorities, residents, businesses, and visitors.

This book begins by outlining the history and development of cities and the development of service science and sustainability science from their early days to the present, while summarizing the main paradigms, concepts, and terminologies in both fields and their reciprocal relationship. It continues by addressing the "what, who, and how" of measuring sustainability, services, and sustainable services, to manage physical and nonphysical resources and tangible and intangible values within the city, and it proposes new concepts and models such as service circularity and sustainable circles to increase the sustainability within and of cities. Finally, it also presents a new model of the service-city, including its architecture and several pertinent examples, which considers it as a platform that manages and integrates the services and systems currently provided by the city while offering additional supporting services to increase the effectiveness of the value and to achieve the goal of sustainability. In addition, it looks ahead to the next generation of municipal models and services and considers how sustainability and services will interact in the cities of the future.

I would first like to thank the series editors, Jim Spohrer and Haluk Demirkan, for offering me the opportunity to write this book. I would also like to thank Patrick Martin for editing the text and assisting me in clarifying my thoughts. At last, I want to acknowledge the generous support of Sami Shamoon College of Engineering, which enabled me to perform the in-depth research in the field of sustainable service that was necessary to complete this book.

—Adi Wolfson

CHAPTER 1

The City Revolution

Today, more than 50 percent of the world's population lives in urban areas, compared to just 3 percent in 1800 and 30 percent in 1950, and that proportion is expected to increase to 66 percent by 2050 (The World Population Prospects 2015). Moreover, populations of the 20 most populated cities in the world increased by 64 percent from 1990 to 2014. Reflecting a similar trend, there were only 83 cities with populations exceeding one million in 1950, and by 2007, this number had risen to 468 (City population Retrieved 2010). In addition, more than 70 percent of the populations of North America and Europe reside in urban areas (Gibson 2007).

But what is a city? The concept of city is very difficult to define. From a social sciences perspective, the simplest and most straightforward definition of a city is a large, often densely populated human settlement that is managed by a distinct local authority that is separate from national authorities (Pile 1999). It is thus also an administrative zone defined according to legal or political boundaries. Furthermore, from architectural and civil engineering perspectives, a city is a space of physical artifacts comprising clusters of buildings, open spaces, public facilities, and infrastructure that are defined within rigid, physical boundaries. In addition, the city is a concentration of public institutions, and it offers trading, health, educational, cultural, and myriad other activities (Larice and Macdonald 2013). As such, it can also be defined as a space of services that are exchanged between a wide variety of stakeholders—namely, residents, traders, visitors, and the city authorities (Frug 1998; Miguel, Tavares, and Araújo 2012). Furthermore, a city is also an active community of continuously interacting people and organizations, and as such, it is defined by economic, social, and cultural boundaries. Finally, it is also an environmental zone that is defined by more dynamic and flexible geographic boundaries, for instance, of climate.

The Origin of Cities

What is the origin of cities, how did they come into existence, and what purposes and functions do they serve? From the dawn of humanity, people were hunter-gatherers, which dictated a nomadic way of life and a reliance on nature's cycles and services, from food, water, and shelter, which are connected to the sowing and ripening cycles and animal migrations, to climate regulation and disease control (i.e., *ecosystem services*, which include provisioning, regulatory, supportive, and cultural services) (Gretchen 1997). Practiced by relatively small groups of people, this lifestyle demanded that group members function together to maintain life. To that end, hunter-gatherers conducted their lives in harmony with the *natural environment*, which is today defined as all the natural (vs. human-made) biotic and abiotic components (i.e., living and nonliving things) that interact in ecosystems. Thus, people of that era focused their energy mainly on maintaining their lives and ensuring the continuity of human life. Similar to humans today, hunter-gatherers had to fulfill their physiological needs for food, water, and air as well as for reproduction and their psychological needs for safety, health, and company. Maslow later defined these requirements as "basic needs" in his hierarchy or pyramid of needs (Maslow 1943).

The beginning of human settlements, attributed mainly to the *Neolithic Revolution* or the first *Agricultural Revolution*, began around 12,000 years ago with the domestication of plants and animals (Barker 2009). Insofar as it changed people's role from solely that of food consumers to also include that of food producers, the first Neolithic Revolution facilitated three major changes in the lifestyle of humans that allowed and even required them to establish permanent settlements: (1) land possession and cultivation; (2) surplus food production, which effectively eliminated the need to wander and to forage for food, but which also required the development of mechanisms of food storage and protection as well as sales and trading services; and (3) population growth engendered by increases in the quantity and availability of food, which also led to increase in the population density in certain regions. These changes led to the establishment of villages that, due to technical limitations, contained at most only a few hundred inhabitants each (Childe 1950). Finally, in addition to driving the shift from a nomadic, hunter-gatherer lifestyle to that based on permanent settlement, the Neolithic Revolution marked the first time not only that people assumed ownership of natural resources (e.g., ground, water, plants, and animals), but also that they interfered with natural systems (e.g., water diversion and accumulation and animal and plant domestication). Moreover, the beginning of permanent settlement also changed the social life and culture of people.

At their most basic level, settlements supplied their inhabitants with a variety of services, from housing and goods provision and storage to protection and trading. They also helped sow the seeds of the *human environment*, which can be defined as an artifact generated by the interactions between human social systems and ecosystems. Nevertheless, several thousand more years were needed to develop the advanced technologies and services, such as water supply and sewage removal systems and governance and cultural services, which characterize cities.

Among the oldest cities on Earth, which—Babylon or Jericho, Athens or Sidon—can be identified as the first official city? Answering this question requires that clearly defined and agreed upon criteria be used to distinguish between a small settlement, a village, and a city. Gordon Childe, who coined the term *Urban Revolution* in 1930, used concepts and theories from the social sciences to interpret archaeological finds. From that perspective, he presented 10 points that characterize the urban revolution and that can be used to define cities (Childe 1936 and 1950).

1. Population number and density. Subsequent researchers proposed that a city is also characterized by the number and density of its residents' houses (Chandler 1987).
2. Characterization and diversity of labor. Though most of the citizens of ancient cities were farmers, other residents adopted new professions, becoming, for example, merchants and guards.
3. Production of capital from taxes that allowed the foundation of authorities.
4. Building of monumental public buildings that symbolized the city, its wealth, and the government.
5. Formation of a ruling class that was in charge of administrative systems.

6. Development of writing systems that enabled the city systems to be recorded and controlled.

7. Development of the sciences and the scientific profession, which facilitated a greater understanding of the world. More importantly, that increase in knowledge enabled people to better predict things and helped accelerate the development of new technologies.

8. Development of the arts and the artistic professions, whose members worked to glorify the wealth and beauty of the city.

9. Development of trade, especially long-distance trade. Most cities settled along established trading routes and became trade centers.

10. Establishment of economic and political communities and more complex social organization.

On the basis of the characteristics stated above, the first cities that conformed to the definition of a "city" were in the region of Mesopotamia, between 4500 and 3100 BCE. Thus the city of Uruk, first settled in circa 4500 BCE, is today considered to have been the first city in the world, followed by Eridu, which was founded in circa 5000 BCE but had grown into a city by circa 2900 BCE.

Evolution of the City

Throughout history, cities have been founded near rivers in fertile areas that were often situated at the intersections of transportation and trade routes, and they served as centers of storage, trade, and manufacturing. Evolutionary analyses of cities distinguish between two main models of city development: (1) cities that grew "naturally" from aggregations of villages and (2) cities that were planned from scratch. In addition, in terms of their physical structure, all cities contained three main elements: (1) buildings, from private housing to municipal structures; (2) networks, such as streets and water supply and sewage systems; and (3) open spaces, some for public activities (e.g., markets) and others merely situated between residential houses and other city facilities to promote the welfare of the citizens (Tertius 1987). Furthermore, for several thousand years, most planned cities adopted a similar plan that comprised a surrounding wall, streets arranged in a grid pattern, and, situated in the city center, a citadel—a structure that, in addition to providing the city's residents with an added level of protection against external threats, was used for a variety of other city functions.

From their origin, cities also supplied many services that can be characterized as nonphysical values or systems; for example, marketplaces, tax systems, and other governance services. Cities also supplied physical security, social order, and continuity (e.g., defense and protection for citizens). Another important aspect of ancient cities comprised the religion services they provided and especially the corresponding establishment of temples. Furthermore, although throughout history cities rose and fell in parallel with empires, their social and economic roles as shelters and administrative zones did not change for hundreds of years.

The populations of ancient cities varied from several thousand at the dawn of cities to 10,000 and even up to 100,000 or more at their pinnacle. In contrast to villages, cities comprised a combination of infrastructures that satisfied their citizens' basic needs, including food and security, services (e.g., trade, health, entertainment), and a community that shared in the social life and culture. These activities correspond to higher levels on Maslow's pyramid (i.e., belonging that is based on friendship and society). In addition, all these needs and functions have constantly shaped and designed the human environment that cities offered, an environment that was constructed mainly from synthetic materials, which effectively erected a barrier between people and nature. In distancing people from nature, this synthetic barrier even effected a disconnection between the two. Eventually, the human environment created by cities and the intensive levels of human activities that took place in and around the cities also altered the natural environment on both local and global scales through unbalanced natural resource utilization and the discharge of human-made materials.

With the start of the *Industrial Revolution* at the end of the 18th century (Lucas 2002), cities grew and changed tremendously. The emergence of new technologies at that time partially replaced tedious hand labor with machine-based employment, enabling agricultural areas to prosper with fewer workers and leading to the establishment of industry in nonagricultural areas. At the beginning of the Industrial Revolution, factories were situated outside the cities, mainly near water sources that were required for the factory machinery. The development of steam power, however, allowed these manufacturing processes to be moved closer to the city centers, in the process spawning massive migrations of people from rural areas to cities. As a result, the bulk of economic, cultural, and governmental systems and facilities became concentrated in cities. Moreover, city architectural design was also revised, and factories, warehouses, and offices were added alongside houses and municipal buildings. In addition, technological innovations that emerged with the Industrial Revolution, from automobile and rail transportation to electricity and telecommunication, changed not only the city landscape but also the lifestyle of people in the cities and the way that cities were operated. Finally, the Industrial Revolution also witnessed the creation of new social classes (e.g., the proletariat, or working class, and the bourgeoisie).

The technological advances that allowed manufacturing processes to be moved within the boundaries of cities were hailed as an advance for civilization, but little thought was devoted to considering the consequences of bringing industrial development closer to the city center. The heavy industrialization that occurred in the cities caused high emissions of pollution, from the release of harmful and toxic gases into the air to the discharge of effluents and solid wastes to the city environment. The reliance on combustion processes in industrial areas in the proximity of city residents eventually created a significant burden on public health. Mainly the result of the air pollution associated with the smoke emanating from factory exhaust pipes, it led to calls for the design of new standards and laws regarding industrial processes.

Several events in the history of industrialization are cited as milestones of the lack of human foresight. In 1952, London was assaulted by the Great Smog event, so named for the heavy smog that smothered the city for four days and eventually caused the deaths of about 4,000 people and injured about 100,000 others. An important datum point in the struggle to significantly reduce London's dangerous air pollution, the Great Smog event spurred similar reactions in other cities around the world. Unfortunately, however, London's Great Smog event has since been followed by environmental catastrophes in other cities. Chief among these are the explosion of chemical facilities in Bhopal, India, in 1984, during which half a million people were exposed to methyl cyanide, a gas whose dissipation killed about 2,500 people, and the Chernobyl nuclear disaster in 1986, where the final total of premature deaths associated with the disaster is estimated at 4,000. In addition to motivating calls for the implementation of more stringent regulations and for the adoption of safety upgrades, these horrific events also highlighted the necessity to remove heavy industry from cities.

The growing city populations spawned the development of social classes that, together with the emerging public transportation systems, resulted in the establishment of suburbs for workers and even neighborhoods in the countryside for the upper classes. Pollution emissions from manufacturing processes also pushed the population from the city center to the suburbs. These residential areas were either part of the city or separate settlements (e.g., villages or small cities) within commuting distance of a city, which allowed people to combine the advantages of city life with the high quality of life, beauty, and tranquility offered by rural areas.

These developments and changes led eventually to the city form with which we are familiar today: a city center that contains business districts and administration buildings paired with a residential suburban area. Despite the many commonalities cities in the world share in terms of their structures and the services they supply, the character and identity of each city is unique due to inherent differences in how it was established and in its developmental path—natural distinctions that arose due to each city's geographic location, climate, wildlife population, and societal characteristics. Likewise, the evolution of each city is inextricably linked with its historical heritage and cultural traditions. For example, while most European cities are very old, many American cities were built virtually from scratch, a process that allowed for their intentional design with the goal of producing more efficient and better cities. Europe is also characterized by a more polycentric and less concentrated urban structure compared with that of the United States. For instance, only 7 percent of the EU population lives in cities of over five million inhabitants, compared with 25 percent in the United States (European Union 2011). In addition, 56 percent of the European urban population lives in small and medium-sized cities and towns of between 5,000 and 100,000 inhabitants. Finally, over the years different types of cities were defined and distinguished, such as the *Capital City*, which is politically important and which usually hosts the government and supreme court of a country, state, or region; the *Mega City* or *Megacity*, a metropolitan area with over 10 million people (initially 8 million); and the *Global City* or *World City*, a city that plays an important role in the global economic system.

The processes of city evolution described above can be illustrated by following the development of New York City, the present-day area of which was already inhabited by Native American tribes in the pre-Columbian era (i.e., the time before Christopher Columbus's first voyage to America in 1492) (Jackson 1995; Homberger and Hudson 2005). The subsequent onset of colonial conquest brought a variety of European voyages to the harbor of New York, and eventually a permanent Dutch settlement named New Amsterdam was established in the 17th century. During the 19th century, New York City was bolstered by waves of European immigration, and it became a trading center. However, the modern city of New York was formed with the consolidation of several cities and counties, such as Brooklyn, the Bronx, Richmond, and Queens in 1898, and by the early 1920s, it became the most populous urbanized area in the world. Moreover, the metropolitan area of the city became the first megacity in human history in the early 1930s (when megacities were still defined as cities with over eight million people). Indeed, from its humble beginnings with a population of about 5,000 in 1689 (Rosenwaike 1972), New York City grew to 60,000 people in 1800 and to 8,550,405 people in 2015 (United States Census Bureau 2016).

Municipal Services

Besides entailing the construction of physical structures, the creation of a city also demanded that city authorities develop the corresponding services the city will need to effectively serve its residents. Initially, these included new municipal services, such as garbage collection, education, and health care systems, but they have since been joined by myriad other services deemed essential to proper functioning of the city. Although differences exist between cities in how they design and offer their respective services, the principal municipal activities offered by most cities today are summarized in Table 1.1.

Table 1.1 **Main municipal services**

Theme	Examples
Civic	Birth, death, and marriage certificates Driving license Legal services
Education	School buildings Education programs Scholarships
Health	Health care system Public health Healthy living
Culture	Historical sites, tours, and so on Parks, galleries, theaters, and so on Sports activities
Social	Welfare system Volunteer support Community activities
Environment	Garbage collection and recycling Air, water, and soil quality Noise control
Transportation	Public transportation Infrastructure Parking
Safety	Police Fire Road
Businesses	Licenses Regulation Support: finance, internships, and so on
Public areas	Gardening, lighting, and so on Development and maintenance of open spaces
Housing	Planning and construction Regulations and licenses Public housing
External relations	National and international partnerships

City Models

The planning, design, and construction sector has a major impact on daily life in the city. In general, the built environment of any urban area is divided into private, commercial, and public areas, all of which include buildings, infrastructure, and open spaces. The bulk of the city area comprises buildings, private and public, and infrastructures. Besides its dominant role in determining the outward appearance of the city, the city's built environment is also responsible for most of the city's resource consumption and waste discharge, from energy consumption and greenhouse gas emissions to water use, wastewater release, and waste generation. Thus, in an attempt to repair the damage of the past and reduce the environmental footprint imposed by the built area of the city, a new construction industry, termed green building, has developed in recent years. Green building is based on the incorporation of environmental aspects during the planning and execution of construction. It also promotes resource conservation and strives to exploit local and recycled materials while considering the region's natural characteristics (e.g., climate and topography). In addition to emphasizing more environmentally friendly building construction, current city development processes stress the creation of urban open spaces such as gardens, parks, green spaces between buildings, ecological corridors, and "urban nature" sites. With their protected biological systems, habitats, and ecosystems, the open spaces in the city play a vital role since they maintain the continuity of the natural systems that benefit biodiversity and that provide services such as rainwater absorption, soil amelioration, and cooling "heat islands," built-up areas that are hotter than nearby rural areas. Moreover, they are social areas that attract people for everything from recreation to leisure to education. At last, in recent years it was also understood that the city should take stringent steps and lead a significant change in the lifestyle of its citizens and visitors, a process that will result in the more rational use of resources within the confines of the city. This will also decrease the ecological footprint of the city (a measure that accounts for the extent to which we exploit natural resources to fulfill our needs and desires, from production of food and clothing to the discharge of wastewater and garbage to leisure time activities, and converts it into equivalent land) and its negative effects on local and global social and natural environments.

Over the years, a variety of new urban models and concepts have been designed and proposed as viable means to reestablish the bond between the human and the natural environments, to increase the quality of life within cities, and to reduce the impacts that cities have on the environment. Some of these models are listed here.

1. **The garden city** is an urban planning model that was proposed at the end of the 19th century in light of increased urbanization and the serious problems it had created, including air pollution, poor sanitary conditions, and social disparities (Buder 1990). The model distinguishes between different land uses in the urban space in an attempt to combine urban construction, rural districts, and industrial areas. Accordingly, residential neighborhoods should be built in a belt around open space that can be used for leisure or for farming, and industrial areas should be located in remote areas far from the city center and from residential areas. The model also includes social and economic dimensions, and it considered the land rights of local residents while calling to divert industrial profits toward urban development. This model was successfully applied at the beginning of the 20th century in Britain and the Netherlands.

2. **City Beautiful Movement** is a philosophy of urban planning that, formulated at the end of the 19th century in North America, takes social, economic, and environmental dimensions into account in a holistic view. The model sought to promote urban beauty not only for the sake of city aesthetics, but also to create new living habits and to instill new social values in the urban environment with the ultimate goal of obtaining better quality of life (Bluestone 1988).

3. **The healthy city** is a model suggested by the World Health Organization that stresses the impact of city activities and policies on human health (Ashton 1991). The model considers health in a broad sense, not only as the absence of disease, but more importantly, as a state of complete physical, mental, and social well-being. It aims to improve and promote a healthy population through health policy and to advance equity and ensure a viable and livable city through the collaboration of its residents, businesses, nongovernmental organizations, and the municipal government.

4. **City liveliness** is a model that defines the place or the most appropriate city in which to live (Coeterier 1994). The liveliness or viability of a city is based on a variety of indicators, among them social

indicators such as security and access to education or health services, economic indicators such as investment in public space and the city's citizens, and environmental indicators such as the volume of green areas, the extent of public transportation, and air and water quality.

5. **Resilient city** is a model that reflects the city's ability to persevere in the event of emergency and to perpetuate its core mission despite the many daunting challenges every city must contend with (Jabareen 2013). Unlike models that aim to reduce the risk in advance, resilience entails the preparation of methodologies, tools, and action plans to deal with the anticipated damage the city could incur from, for example, natural or human-generated disasters. As such, the resilient city model, instead of focusing only on preventing climate change, will also include plans for coping with the effects of future climate change, such as floods, influxes of refugees, and invasive animal species.

6. **Regenerative city** is a model that conceptualizes the city as a closed system that provides and renews all the resources needed by the city to enable it to address the environmental, social, and economic risks associated with cities (Girardet 2017). This model is driven by the goal of enabling the consumption of local resources while finding ways to regenerate them without harming the social or natural environment.

Many recent studies in the broad field of city science focus on two main visions and action plans: the **Smart City** (Caragliu, Del Bo and Nijkamp 2011; Townsend 2013) and the **Sustainable City** (Satterthwaite 1997; Lehmann 2010; Newman and Jennings 2012). The notion of the smart city refers to the integration of solutions based on information and communication technology (ICT) and the Internet of Things (IoT) to manage city resources, services, and assets. Born of the *Information Revolution*, the smart city model tremendously changed the way people manage cities, and as such, it affects all of us on a daily basis. The smart city envisions connecting people, services, and infrastructures via ICT and its applications to promote better utilization of data and improve organizational performance, thereby facilitating more efficient decision-making processes. The smart city action plan is divided into six major areas (Wolfson 2016): (1) smart governance through democracy, transparency, and public sharing; (2) smart economy based on the local economy, green growth (i.e., economic growth that also ensures overall civilian well-being together with environmental equity and benefits), and increased competitiveness; (3) smart mobility through the use of sophisticated transport systems and traffic management; (4) smart environment through environmental monitoring, conservation of resources, and reduction of the city's environmental footprint; (5) smart living through implementation of health systems, social services, and smart homes; and (6) smart people by developing extensive education and training resources that answer the needs of all citizens.

The sustainable city was conceptualized as an integration of quality of life and environmental concerns with social justice and local and agglomeration economies. It aims to ensure the rich and fair existence of its citizens, to provide them with a wide range of benefits, and to promote the overall prosperity of the city while using physical and nonphysical resources rationally and equitably and assuming responsibility at the local and global levels over the short and the long term. In practice, it refers to how the city's resources are used and how environmental damage is minimized while imposing certain limits on social and economic activities. The sustainable city incorporates and promotes the following general qualities: (1) well-being—ensure physical, mental, social, economic, and environmental quality of life for individuals and groups; (2) diversity—promote equal rights and an inclusive atmosphere that encourages different communities to settle in the city; (3) equity—ensure equal rights and opportunities and the fair division of the city's resources; (4) rational use of resources—from reductions in the use of city resources to the design of methods to promote renewability; and (5) cooperation—cooperation and collaboration between all city stakeholders that encourages their active involvement and that cultivates in them a sense of responsibility.

The smart city and sustainable city models have much in common, as the smart city aims to promote sustainable development and the sustainable city exploits smart solutions. In addition, both models strive to develop and implement plans for saving resources, to design efficient physical and nonphysical systems to improve urban development, and to manage and increase civic engagement and public participation in the city. However, while technology that reshapes and advances city services is at the core of the smart city, the sustainable city is more about the integration of responsible and shared economic, social, and environmental values that, in turn, will generate better city services. Moreover, the smart city employs physical infrastructures that benefit the community whereas the sustainable city refers to the people and their community that use the infrastructure for their common good. Furthermore, while the smart city model is currently applied mainly in the design and implementation of solutions in existing cities without altering the present forms of these cities, sustainable city solutions deal more with the redesign and development of cities to obtain the desired results. Yet the main difference between the two models is that "smart" relates to increased efficiency while "sustainability" relates to wisdom and to increased effectiveness (Ackoff 1989).

The City of Tomorrow

What will tomorrow's cities look like? Notwithstanding the difficulties associated with forecasting the future and envisioning how cities will develop and change in the coming decades, volumes of research have been devoted to the future of cities and the cities of the future (Etezadzadeh 2015; Jenks and Jones 2009; Flint and Raco 2012; Nam and Pardo 2011; Axhausen et al. 2012; Khodabakhsh, Fathi and Mashayekhi 2016; Ratti and Claudel 2016; European Union 2011).

Today, cities are agglomerations of the world's main economic, social, and cultural activities. Yet the modern city is not merely a collection of buildings, roads, parks, and public institutions and a corresponding set of services, but a dynamic space of people, infrastructure, and services that are interconnected and jointly creating the active, living entity of the city (Wolfson 2016). Collectively, modern cities play a major role in national and global processes, such as economic growth, and they lead civil and environmental revolutions in the world; for example, promote the solar energy revolution. Of course, the city of the future can be envisioned in myriad ways, and as such, it is vitally important that each city be planned and developed based on the needs of its inhabitants and its other stakeholders while considering its local resources and its legacy. Yet various global processes such as global warming should be considered when building future cities from scratch and in the redesign of current cities to ensure that they will be able to effectively meet the anticipated challenges of the future, including but not limited to (1) increased consumption levels that could negatively affect the availability of natural resources and the health of the environment; (2) advances in technology, particularly the development of the digital world; (3) changes in the work environment (e.g., working remotely) and in the labor market, including the shift from markets based on agriculture and manufacturing to services-based markets and the increased use of machines and robots in place of people; (4) changes in the balance between the time we spend in private versus public spaces and how we use those spaces; (5) emergence of the *share economy* (also termed *shareconomy*), in which the ownership of resources, assets, goods, and services is replaced by access; and (6) emergence of service dominant logic (SDL), a paradigm that views service provision rather than product exchange as being at the core of each exchange and that promotes the joint cocreation of value by a provider and a customer.

To ensure that tomorrow's cities will be equipped to cope with these challenges, future city design approaches should be based on exploiting the inherent values of the city's fundamental building blocks—its people, infrastructures, and services—and on revising, vis-à-vis city functions, their respective roles and the connections between them. A good city design process will not only be driven by a broad, long-term vision of what kind of city its planners envision—more importantly, it will require the active involvement of its residents in all decision making relevant to city planning, and it will encourage its residents to assume responsibility for the space in which they live. In this respect, the community as a whole is a much more powerful agent for the implementation and maintenance of change than are the city's individual citizens. Another important issue in the design and development of future cities is decoupling of economic and social growth from the qualities of life and environment.

1

CHAPTER 2

Sustainability and Service

To fulfill the vision of cities—that they provide high quality of life for their residents and promote their prosperity, that they support flourishing economies and healthy and rich social and natural environments—cities should focus on developing and integrating the two key concepts of services and sustainability. In this context, services refers to interactions between people, infrastructure, and systems that ultimately confer on the city intangible values, and sustainability relates to the integration of social, environmental, and economic values to maintain the social and natural environments but from a broad and future-oriented perspective (Dresner 2008).

Sustainability

The mutual relations between humanity and the environment have undergone vast change since the appearance of the first humans on Earth. Since then, evolutionary and revolutionary processes have continuously reshaped the interaction between people and their surroundings. Moreover, the advent of powerful new technologies, which have helped drive substantial social and cultural change, have repeatedly redefined the interplay between humankind and nature and the role that each party plays in this relationship.

During the long period in which people were hunter-gatherers, humans had a harmonious and symbiotic relationship with nature—people adapted their lives to the cycles of nature and were an integral part of ecosystems. That relationship changed little until about 70,000 years ago, when the *Language Revolution*, also known as the Cognitive Revolution, led to the development of consciousness, conscience, and a new perception of reality, and in so doing, it drove immense social change (Mellars and Stringer 1989). In parallel with their physical needs, people also began to allocate time and space to their emotional needs, but these were not necessarily directly related to nature. It was not until the Agricultural Revolution that people first intentionally altered the natural environment through their domestication of plants and animals as well as their selection and designation of some land areas to agriculture and others to permanent settlements (Barker 2009). Not only did people redesign the natural environment, they also built a human environment. But perhaps the most significant change in the relationship between humanity and the environment occurred in the wake of the Industrial Revolution, which ushered in the wide-scale use of novel technologies that, in turn, fostered significant social advances as well as the massive exploitation of natural resources to the benefit of humankind but to the detriment of ecosystems and biodiversity. Moreover, since the Industrial Revolution, human society has continued to pursue new, advanced, and more efficient technologies to expand the capabilities and superiority of the human race. These developments have effectively enabled humankind to master nature, but in so doing, humans have inflicted undue harm on their planet, deepening the ever-growing rift between the natural and the human environments.

The beginnings of environmental ideology can be traced to the *Scientific Revolution*, which fostered the development of scientific research when it emerged in the 16th century during the early modern period. Yet the seeds of this philosophy, as it is known today, were effectively buried at the end of the 18th century with the rise of the *Romantic Movement*, an intellectual and artistic movement that conceived of nature and of all people as nonrecurring and unique. Philosophers and artists during this period highlighted the beauty and power of nature and the importance of inculcating the "wonder of nature" in people. They also extolled the human connection to nature and called for a "return to nature" while reconsidering humankind's relationship with its planet's natural environment. This romantic notion of nature developed, in part, as a reaction to the accelerated rates of industrialization and urbanization that characterized the period and that were faulted for the seemingly increased detachment of the human environment from its natural surroundings. During this period, people began to cultivate an ecocentric perspective of the natural world that assigns equal importance to the living and non-living components of ecosystems and that stresses the place of people as an integral component of nature. The ecocentric perspective developed in response to the anthropocentric perception—according to which humans can intervene in and control natural processes—that took root during the same period.

The science of *ecology*, which investigates the interactions between organisms and their environment (Odum, Odum, and Andrews 1971), was developed at the beginning of the 19th century, when the ideas of conservation and preservation began to attract more attention. Furthermore, the nascent global conservation efforts of that time have driven the establishment of myriad nature reserves and conservation organizations and societies. Looking back, however, one could conclude that overall, conservation has been a failure. Although conservation ideas have been successfully applied in many different parts of the world, there is still an artificial separation between natural areas or nature reserves and areas where there is human activity, such as cities or industrial zones.

Although efforts to preserve the natural environment and wildlife constituted the driving force behind the establishment of environmental movements, they were only partially responsible for the development of environmental ideology. The great economic recession of the 1980s generated new questions about the social order and about the common values held by society and about the role and necessity of industry along with the role and necessity of nature. This stage in the development of environmental ideology and the environmental movement was characterized by efforts to understand the troubling findings of research in the fields of ecology and conservation. The growing realization that human activity was linked with a slew of environmental problems fueled debates about the health risks associated with the Industrial Revolution and urbanization, in the process sowing the seeds of the first civil models of *public health* and *environmental quality* that emerged later. Central to those debates was the perception that the by-products of industrial processes, including the production of solid waste and effluents and the emission of gases to the air, were having deleterious effects on human health (i.e., an anthropocentric approach).

The antiwar *Flower Child Movement* of the 1960s was a key driving factor in the establishment of local and international organizations and movements that put the natural environment at the center of their doctrines (e.g., Friends of the Earth (1969) and Greenpeace (1970)). These groups not only focused on preserving the natural environment and opposed the development and growth of cities, they also protested against the use of nuclear energy, a protest that was coupled with the earlier campaigns against the use of nuclear weapons. In 1970, Richard Nixon founded the U.S. Environmental Protection Agency (EPA) after the United States declared a national environmental policy and began to promote legislation to ameliorate damage to the environment. Since its inception, the agency, which later became a model for similar bodies established in many other countries, has played a significant role in protecting the environment.

The 1960s and 1970s also constituted a time when the multidisciplinary field of *environmental science*, which combines knowledge from various areas of the natural sciences and incorporates elements of the human-environment interface, was developed as a separate discipline of science. Moreover, a mature environmental ideology emerged during this period, as did a plethora of new environmental models with broader outlooks that combined philosophical and moral dimensions with strong scientific backgrounds. Such models include, for instance, green building (US Green Building Council 2009), eco-fashion (Niinimäki 2010), and even ecopoetry (Bryson 2002). As these approaches gained momentum, they helped spawn additional models—such as the *Gaia theory* or the *Gaia hypothesis* (Kirchner 2002) and *deep ecology* (Pepper 2002)—that emphasize the intrinsic value of all nature's components, biotic and abiotic. At their most basic level, these new environmental philosophies implored humans to rethink their behavior and to thoroughly restructure their lives around a more holistic vision of the natural environment and their place in it. Insofar as they undermined and threatened the prevailing notion of humanity's centrality in the universe, however, these controversial models have generated bitter criticism and wide opposition that continue until today.

Throughout the 20th century and into the 21st, people's awareness that their actions have extensive and far-reaching consequences, particularly vis-à-vis the natural environment, has been growing. Moreover, it was understood that positive environmental change cannot be achieved without simultaneously considering social needs—for example, issues of welfare and social justice—in a manner that also yields economic benefits and growth. This understanding led to the development of the model of *sustainability*, which has its roots in the 1970s (Dresner 2008). Sustainability refers generally to the capacity to perpetuate the stable continuation of natural processes and procedures over time by constantly integrating and assessing their environmental, social, and economic dimensions while accentuating their interconnectedness or interdependencies. In short, it strives to achieve balance, or equilibrium, between the ability of nature to sustain natural systems (e.g., natural cycles, food chains, ecosystems, etc.) and its capacity to support life and the development and needs of a specific population, human or otherwise, that depends on these processes.

Since the notion of sustainability first appeared in the 1970s, vast efforts have been invested in elucidating the concept and in framing it in terms that people can easily understand. Thus, sustainability is about how to live today so that subsequent generations can enjoy at least the same conditions. It bridges between body and soul, combining intelligence, feeling, knowledge, love, and care to attain comprehensive, long-range planning that simultaneously accounts for the continuity of the economic, social, and environmental dimensions of life. Sustainability involves the integration of numerous fields and factors in ensuring the ability of processes and states of a system to endure. Thus, it has to be taken into account on a daily basis and requires continuous learning and creative adaptation to confront the varied changes inherent in life. The processes that are involved in maintaining sustainability, therefore, are relatively complex and not straightforward. Accordingly, one of the main obstacles to practically applying sustainability's concepts involves transitioning the philosophy from theory to practice. Its practical application includes, in part, dissecting the theoretical concepts and redefining them in terms of more practical, visible, and accessible values, measures, methods, and tools.

One of the most well-developed methods used today to pursue the goal of sustainability in practice is *sustainable development*. The principle of sustainable development was introduced in 1987 by the Brundtland Commission, established by the World Commission on Environmental Conservation and Development (WCED) of the United Nations, in its groundbreaking report entitled *Our Common Future*. According to the

Brundtland Commission, sustainable development is that which "meets the needs of the present without compromising the ability of future generations to meet their own needs" (Brundtland 1987). Simply put, applying the principle of sustainable development dictates that developmental processes be designed in cyclical rather than linear terms such that the rate of resource utilization does not outpace that of resource renewal. To ensure that sustainable development achieves workable, stable, and equitable outcomes, it must integrate environmental considerations, social and economic knowledge, engineering and natural sciences, and the humanities and social sciences. In addition, sustainable development takes into account all potential short- and long-term effects at both the local and the global scales, and it is necessarily inclusive, involving every stakeholder, from individuals to whole societies (Figure 2.1).

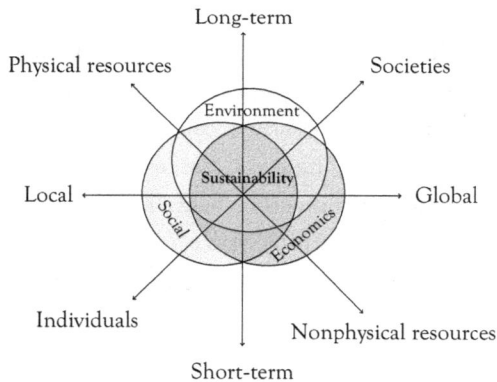

Figure 2.1 Components of sustainability (Wolfson 2016)

Service

Almost as old as humankind, the concept of service is described by four general characteristics, as summarized in Table 2.1.

Traditionally, service has been defined according to the value-in-exchange model as an intangible value delivered from a supplier who produces the value to a consumer who uses it (Figure 2.2a) (Wolfson et al. 2015; Maglio, Kieliszewski, and Spohrer 2010). In this traditional service marketing view, services are simultaneously produced and delivered, yet the value-in-exchange model resembles the production and delivery

Table 2.1 Service characteristics

Characteristic	Explanation
Intangibility	Service can be neither seen nor touched, and it is based mainly on nonphysical resources.
Inseparability	Service is simultaneously produced, delivered, and consumed, thereby requiring direct interaction between the supplier and the consumer.
Perishability	Services cannot be stored; all tangible and intangible resources and systems involved in supplying a service are used for a limited time during service delivery.
Heterogeneity	Service cannot be repeated in exactly the same way each time it is performed, as it depends not only on the supplier and the client, but also on the place and the time of provision.

of tangible values within a traditional goods-driven economy (i.e., the production and delivery of goods, a process that is usually performed in two sequential steps). With the increasing importance of services in our lives and the emergence of new technological tools (mainly information and communication technologies), the service sector became an increasingly dominant force in the economy and spurred the development of the *service-dominant logic* paradigm (Vargo and Lusch 2004; Lush and Vargo 2006; Vargo, Maglio, and Akaka 2008). Describing economies as fundamentally based on services and goods that function as distribution mechanisms for service provision, this paradigm replaces the goods-dominant logic that focused on industrial-based products or manufacturing outputs. As such, service-dominant logic was conceptualized as analogous to ecosystem services to emphasize the importance of the intangible value that services provide to the economy. Vargo and Lush also suggested 10 foundational premises to define the framework of service-dominant logic (Vargo and Lusch 2004). Furthermore, service-dominant logic integrates marketing, the management of resources, and the value chain, and it redefines the primary unit of exchange, the determination and meaning of value, the role of the customer, and the nature of provider-customer interaction (Aitken et al. 2006). In the frame of this paradigm, the value-in-exchange model prominent in the goods-dominant economy was replaced by the value-in-use model (Figure 2.2b), according to which providers and customers work together—often via a platform maintained

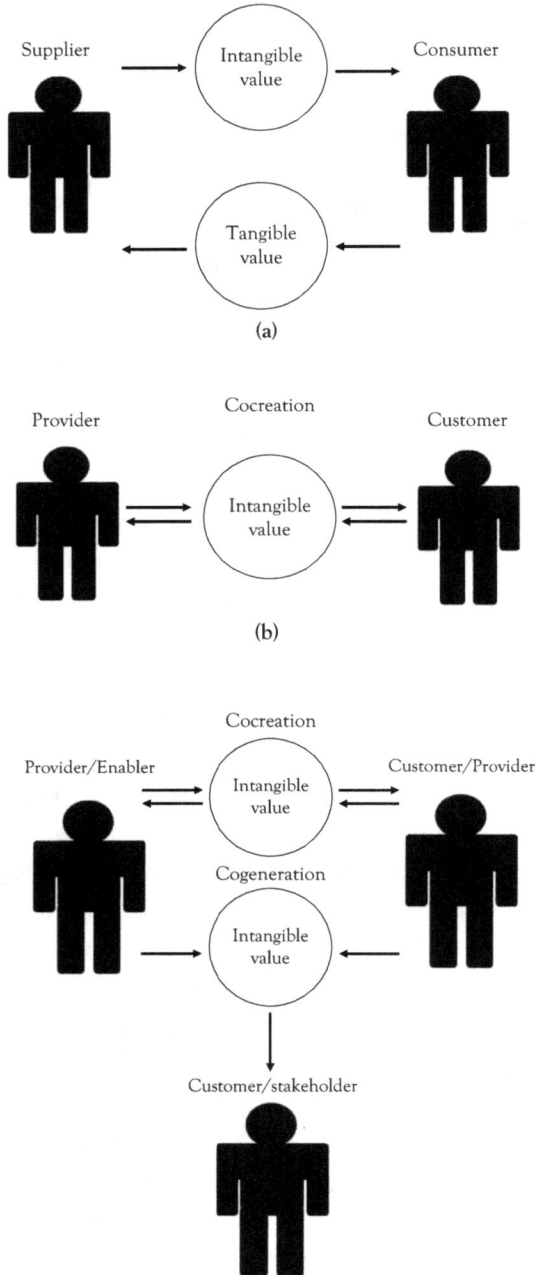

Figure 2.2 Service production and delivery models: (a) value-in-exchange, (b) value-in-use, and (a) value-in-return

by the provider for the benefit of customer interaction with the service—on the cocreation of value. Moreover, in this model all parties invest their own resources, facilities, and efforts, as well as the information and knowledge at their disposal, in the production and delivery of value.

In general, value can be cocreated at three different levels that are defined according to how the service is designed and performed. Thus, value can be cocreated at the levels of (i) cousage, when customers exploit a service and passively cocreate value by creating the perception of value (e.g., using public transportation), (ii) coperformance or coproduction, when customers partially share in performing the tasks required to deliver the service (e.g., bill payment via an Internet site or application), and (iii) codesign, where a dialog between customers and service providers determines the types and forms of service that are desired (e.g., design of education services with students). Furthermore, value can be cocreated through various modes that are differentiated according to the extent to which each actor—provider or customer—is responsible for supplying the resources and effort needed to perform the service. These modes include (i) self-service, based mainly on investment by the customer (e.g., booking a hotel via the Internet), (ii) super-service, where providers are the main investors (e.g., ordering a delivery from the supermarket), and (iii) mixed-service, which relies on more balanced investments by the two groups (e.g., using a travel agency to book a flight) (Campbell, Maglio and Davis 2011; Wolfson, Tavor, and Mark 2012). Additionally, in some cases value cocreation can be extended to a value-in-return model, according to which customers also become the providers of either the same or a complementary value that they cogenerate with the provider, who is also known as an enabler, for the benefit of other customers (Figure 2.2c) (Wolfson 2016).

To create value, service provision relies on the performance of myriad activities that depend on both provider and customer and that together constitute the service value chain. However, as most services are not stand-alone entities, they are provided in conjunction with other tangible and intangible values as part of a service system (Spohrer et al. 2008) or even as part of a service network (Allee 2008) that comprises multiple service systems (i.e., system of service systems). In addition, the service atmosphere can be enclosed within physical or nonphysical boundaries in a self-contained framework that provides customers with all the services they need, (e.g., a cruise ship), and as such, it is defined as a whole service (Demirkan, Spohrer, and Krishna 2011). Finally, when all the services of a system are provided in concert to maintain quality of life for some extended period of time in a highly efficient and effective manner, the service atmosphere or constellation is considered a holistic service system (Demirkan, Spohrer, and Krishna 2011; Spohrer, Piciocchi, and Bassano 2012).

Insofar as it provides "whole service" to its primary population of people (e.g., nation, state, city, household or family farm, etc.), a holistic service system is independent of all external service systems and is capable of functioning for an extended period of time while balancing independence with interdependence (e.g., limit outsourcing, recycle to conserve resources, etc.). The holistic service system thus provides the people inside the service entity access to "whole service," including transportation, water, food, energy, communications, buildings, retail, finance, health, education, governance, and so on (Spohrer, Piciocchi, and Bassano 2012).

In parallel with the emergence of service-dominant logic, IBM initiated research into service and social engineering systems, coining the field *service science*. To clearly define the goal of service science and to promote service innovation, IBM launched a multidisciplinary academic endeavor it termed *service science, management, and engineering (SSME)* (IBM Almaden Services Research 2006). Several years later, when service became more complex and comprehensive and necessarily involved numerous disciplines and stakeholders, service science became a platform for the systematic study, development, and implementation of services and innovation (Spohrer et al. 2007; Maglio and Spohrer 2007; Maglio, Kieliszewski, and Spohrer 2010).

Sustainable Service

The fundamentals of sustainable service and the strategies for making a service more sustainable are still in development. As previously stated by Henriques and Richardson (2004), the main challenge facing sustainability efforts is to advance beyond the mere realization of eco-efficient products and processes toward achieving *triple-bottom-line* solutions that include social and environmental dimensions with the economic measures traditionally evaluated in bottom-line assessments of performance.

Wolfson et al. (2010) recently presented a novel perspective on sustainability, including a model that describes the relationship between sustainability and service within the framework of service science. In that work, sustainable service was defined not only as a service that fulfills customer demands and that has minimal impact on both the natural and the social environments, but also as a service that incorporates sustainability as a basic value and as an essential part of value production and delivery. The model therefore suggests that a sustainable service should imbue each phase of the service value chain with sustainability (Figure 2.3) while considering all stakeholders, from today's suppliers to the generations of tomorrow. It should also engender a fundamental shift in the traditional roles of the primary participants in the service. Thus, the service supplier becomes a provider, and the consumer assumes the role of customer. These new roles are defined by a value cocreation process, in which value is produced and used jointly and reciprocally by the provider and the customer.

In the frame of the new model, the value cocreation process involves value chains. Each value chain should be seen as a combination of a *core-value*, or the essence of the solution that a certain service provides and that should be cocreated and delivered from a provider to a customer, and a *super-value*, or the generation of other values, supporting

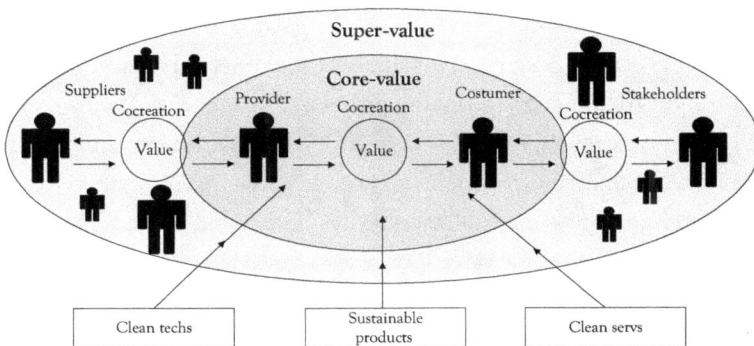

Figure 2.3 Sustainable service (Wolfson 2016)

and complementary to the core-value, via additional direct and indirect suppliers and customers (Figure 2.3). Simply put, the value chain of a sustainable service is initiated by suppliers who cocreate the super-value with the provider. The provider then cocreates the core-value with the customer while simultaneously considering the cocreation of super-value with other stakeholders, which include subsequent generations. In this model, all value production and delivery stages along the value chain are based on the rational use of resources and on the efficient utilization of sustainable products. Fundamental to a sustainable service, both rational resource use and efficiency can be promoted by the design and implementation of cleantechs, or clean technologies aimed at streamlining production with respect to resource use and reducing the output of by-products and pollution (Pernick and Wilder 2007), and CleanServs, service-based solutions that are competitive with, if not superior to, their conventional, tangible or intangible counterparts by preventing, reducing, replacing, streamlining (i.e., efficiency), or offsetting the production of goods and services (Wolfson, Tavor, and Mark 2013, 2014; Wolfson et al. 2015). Furthermore, in addition to mitigating environmental risks and damage, sustainable services will also generate tangible benefits in the form of more efficient use of natural resources. Finally, in addition to its applicability to the traditional service sector, the new perspective and its accompanying model can also serve as a framework for entrepreneurship and innovation in the research and practice of both service and sustainability to generate new and alternative values and supply customer demands more sustainably.

Insofar as services are not separate entities and they interact with other values and processes to achieve the service goal, it is also imperative that sustainable service design be integrated with other services and manufacturing, agricultural, and mining processes. To that end, Wolfson et al. (2010) proposed a new model, termed "S^3—sustainability and services science," which describes sustainable service as the integration of physical and nonphysical resources and tangible and intangible values (Figure 2.4). Thus, the model of sustainable service comprises two main stages: first, a sustainable decision made by a service, with said decision relying on the service's resources, including natural resources, technologies, and information and knowledge; second, the most sustainable choice is selected

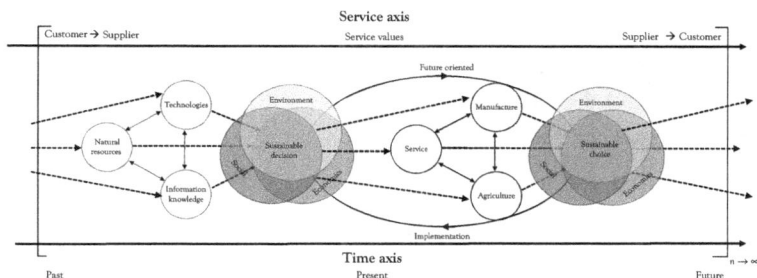

Figure 2.4 S³—Sustainability and services science model (Wolfson et al. 2010)

from among the alternatives after evaluating each in terms of its integration of services and manufacturing and agricultural processes (Wolfson et al. 2010).

In contrast to the case for manufacturing and agricultural processes, for a service joint and reciprocal value cocreation is a fundamental prerequisite, and, therefore, sustainability should also be an integral part of the interactions among providers and beneficiaries. This means that the provider-customer relationship must advance beyond simply sharing in the responsibilities for the physical and nonphysical resources (e.g., knowledge, skills, efforts, and capabilities) to include a sustainable division between provider and customer of all resources and tasks associated with the service. From this perspective, the decision of which service mode to choose (e.g., *self-service* or *e-service*) is also important. For example, withdrawing money from a bank can be done in a self-service fashion using an ATM, eliminating the need to physically visit a teller at a bank, which requires significantly more facilities and resources. Likewise, bills can be paid using an e-service for a more sustainable alternative than driving to the post office or to the bank.

Achieving the goal of sustainable service can also be promoted by adopting a natural mimicry approach, which entails designing service systems based on the so-called rules of nature (Wolfson, Tavor, and Mark 2011). Simply put, these rules dictate the rational use of resources and the implementation of energy efficiency measures, the adoption of future-oriented and life cycle perspectives, and the ability to adapt smoothly to changes in an evolutionary fashion. In addition, because the production of goods is inherently tied to natural resource use and associated with the discharge to the environment of various by-products, the production and delivery of a solution based on an intangible value (i.e., service) is preferred from the perspective of sustainability.

Sustainability as Service

Sustainability itself is an intangible value that is produced and delivered simultaneously (i.e., inseparable), that can neither be stored nor returned (i.e., perishable), and whose overall appearance or performance depends on the time and place of provision and on both the provider and the customer (i.e., heterogeneous). As such, it is in fact a service par excellence (Wolfson et al. 2015), and like a service, its intangibility and perishability signify that it cannot be seen, touched, or stored. Indeed, this is also one of the main reasons why it is so difficult to comprehend the meaning of sustainability and, more importantly, that its implementation is such a challenge.

Treating sustainability as a service, however, greatly simplifies the process and will allow the philosophy and ideas behind sustainability to be put into practice (e.g., methods, tools, etc.) while simultaneously conceptualizing a clearer and more concrete definition of sustainability. Approaching sustainability as a service dictates primarily that the provider/ providers, the customer/customers, and the value be clearly specified and that actions be taken to gain insight into the components of the value chain. It also obliges the provider to design and develop a value that can be delivered and that can eventually be used by the customer. In addition, it encourages the formation of a value cocreation process between the provider and the customer, built on the efficient use of both physical and nonphysical resources and on the correct division of those resources between the two actors. In the long-term framework of sustainability, the customer is eventually recruited to be a provider of sustainability to other stakeholders (i.e., super-service), including those in the next generation. Finally, by defining sustainability as a service, both the idea and the practice of sustainability can be advanced.

CHAPTER 3

What, Who, and How to Measure

Measuring, one of the basic tools to control, manage, and improve processes, also facilitates making comparisons between alternatives to any given process. Moreover, the data generated by measurements supports planning and decision-making processes with pertinent knowledge to yield more efficient and applicable solutions. To obtain significant data that accurately portrays a given process under analysis, however, relies decisively on the task of defining what to measure and how it should be measured, a challenge to some extent in any measurement endeavor.

In general, indicators that correspond to a creation parameter or property or to a value derived therein (e.g., concentration in air of particulate matter, carbon monoxide, sulfur dioxide, or nitrogen dioxide) can be used to assess and quantify a particular situation (Wolfson 2016). Yet indicators are usually narrow and specific. Thus, indexes that integrate several indicators and that also account for the relative importance of each are also employed. A widely used example is that of air quality index, or air pollution index, which accounts for several major air pollutants. Moreover, in contrast to indicators, which are narrow and specific by definition, indexes convey more information and, in certain cases, more knowledge. In terms of sustainability measures that account for economic, social, and environmental indicators and indexes, efforts to combine multiple indicators into a single, comparative number are ongoing.

Although indexes attempt to describe given situations on the basis of the indicators they contain, not all measures are suitable to illustrate every system or process. Thus, while some measures are strong indicators and are highly sensitive in one case, in another case they provide almost no information whatsoever. We can also differentiate between the measurement of physical and nonphysical resources and tangible and intangible values. In contrast to the typically straightforward and accessible nature of physical resource measures, the measurement of nonphysical values is qualitative in some cases and quantitative in others. Qualitative assessments are used to elucidate the underlying reasons, opinions, and motivations and to provide insights vis-à-vis the problem. On the other hand, quantitative assessments are used to quantify the problem by generating data that can be transformed into usable numbers or statistics, and in so doing they quantify attitudes, opinions, behaviors, and other defined variables (Neuman and Robson 2012). Finally, all measures can be assessed at the micro or macro level. Micro-level measurements consider the various entities in the process's supply chain, while macro-level measurements refer to the process as a whole.

Physical Resource Measures

Virtually any system or process can be assessed with physical resource measures that, when combined to create indexes, constitute a fundamental economic tool that can also be applied to environmental assessments. Physical resource measures include not only the amounts of resources extracted from the environment to run a process (i.e., inputs), but also the volume of materials discharged from the process to the surroundings (i.e., outputs). The assessment can be performed by considering the system's inputs and outputs (i.e., by performing mass and energy balances) at both the micro and macro levels. Moreover, it is applicable to a good, a service, a process, or a city, and in many methodologies it is termed material flow analysis or resource flow analysis (Narayanaswamy et al. 2003).

When done to assess the sustainability of a system, a resource flow analysis is usually expressed in terms of the ecological, carbon, and water footprints. Ecological footprint is a measure of the area of productive land required to supply human demands and to absorb the impact of human activity on nature (Wackernagel and Rees 1998). It is calculated by summing the total area of cropland, grazing land, forest, and fishing grounds required not only to produce the energy, food, fiber, and synthetic products used by humans for housing and infrastructure as well as for leisure activities, but also to absorb the corresponding waste and polluting emissions. Carbon footprint is a measure of greenhouse gas emissions over the course of the entire value chain of a product, whether it is a good or a service, and today, it is one of the most widely used sustainability measures. Encompassing the product's entire life cycle, the carbon footprint is based on the total energy and materials used over that life cycle, from the mining and extraction of the raw materials to the end of the product's life (Weidema et al. 2008). Similarly, water footprint is a measure of the amount of water consumed by a process, and it includes direct water use (e.g., tap water, rivers, etc.) and indirect water use (e.g., green water, or naturally occurring ground water that also contributes to crop growth) (Aldaya 2012).

Life Cycle Assessment

One useful method for performing a resource flow analysis (i.e., input-output inventory and mass and energy balance) is life cycle assessment or analysis (LCA). A dissection of all the stages that constitute the life cycle of each good or service from "cradle to grave" (i.e., from creation to disposal) or from "cradle to cradle" (i.e., waste-free life cycle), LCA monitors the resources that were utilized and discharged at each stage and over the entire course of the life cycle of the product or service (Day 1981; Finnveden et al. 2009). As such, the negative and positive impacts on environmen can be measured and monitored. The data collected can then be applied to streamline the product life cycle, in the process reducing its negative effects relative to its positive impacts at the social and environmental levels. Similar to its use at the micro level to assess a product's life cycle, the LCA methodology can also be applied at the macro level to the activities and services associated with entire cities.

Although there are already agreed-upon sets of criteria and procedures to define the goals of an LCA—which are to examine the inputs and outputs of materials and energy throughout the product life cycle and to define the relevant measures for decision making—the methodology also has some limitations owing primarily to the absence of nonphysical or intangible values (e.g., effort, equity, or accessibility) from its calculation. To address this shortcoming, the United Nations offered a general model, the life cycle sustainability assessment (LCSA), which offers a more holistic view of the product life cycle. Its comprehensive nature owes to the inclusion in the LCSA of the positive and negative impacts on the environmental, social, and economic perspectives of decision-making processes to guide stakeholders toward the choice of more sustainable products based on analyses that encompass the products' entire life cycles (Finkbeiner 2010).

As such, the LCSA sums the results of the environmental life cycle assessment, the social life cycle assessment, and the life cycle costs to help clarify the trade-offs between the three pillars of sustainability (economic, social, and environmental), with the ultimate goal of helping decision makers choose the most sustainable value of each product.

Environmental Life Cycle Assessment (E-LCA)

In the years since its inception, the LCA concept has been adapted to address different aspects of the pillars of sustainability. To evaluate the potential environmental impacts of a product or a process over the entire course of its life cycle, the environmental LCA (E-LCA) was conceived. The outcome of an E-LCA can promote the design or redesign of more environmentally friendly products and the implementation of practical technological solutions (Jolliet 2015).

Similar to LCA, the E-LCA is equally applicable to the assessment of both products and services and their interaction. For example, the E-LCA of food with respect to water and energy use is a commonly used method to compare not only different products, but also different producers. The life cycles of food products, especially those of vegetables and fruit, utilize large amounts of natural resources, such as the water and nutrients directly involved in their cultivation. Furthermore, they also contribute to the emission of greenhouse gases (Yang and Campbell 2017). Perhaps the most well-known index of greenhouse gas emissions is the carbon footprint, the main contributors to which in the typical life cycle of a food product are the transportation of the food from the supplier to the consumer and, to grow the food, the provision of water through mechanized pumping systems. In addition, the carbon footprint of food also incorporates gases attributed to the use of fertilizers and to other farming-related activities associated with agriculture. (e.g., agricultural machinery, warehouse energy, etc.)

In today's global economy, a large portion of the carbon footprint of produce is due to its transportation, which in many cases involves shipment to one or more central distribution points before the farm products make it to the market. The carbon footprint of produce can therefore be significantly reduced by obtaining fruit and vegetable products from local growers, thereby eliminating the need for transportation and reducing the amount of energy used by the conventional distribution network (Wright and Hollingshead 2011). This goal can be achieved not only by offering subsidies to local farmers, but also by encouraging farmers to sell directly to consumers or use food cooperatives. Alternatively, carbon footprint of produce can also be reduced by establishing community gardens. Not only do they yield local produce and promote a sense of community through the shared interest and participation in cultivating a garden, community gardens can also reduce the life cycle footprint of vegetables. Moreover, community gardens also add social impact to the process and effectively redesign the entire process of agricultural production as a service. In addition to fostering community identity and increasing the sense of community ownership and stewardship, community gardens also have economic benefits related mainly to food production. Furthermore, they also have environmental benefits, from beautifying the urban environment and connecting people with nature to the use of rainwater, production of oxygen, cleansing of the air, and the capture of carbon dioxide. In light of these numerous potential benefits, recent years have witnessed an increase in the number of community services departments in cities that have implemented plans to encourage their residents to create community gardens by offering assistance in their design, development, and maintenance.

To empirically determine the extent to which community gardens can reduce the carbon footprint of produce, Issac and Brown (2016) compared the LCA of conventionally grown lettuce with that of lettuce grown in community gardens and measured the carbon footprint of the produce in both scenarios. They found that the total emission of conventionally grown California lettuce 0.7 $kg_{eq}CO_2/kg$ was halved to 0.35 $kg_{eq}CO_2/kg$ by growing the crop in a community garden ($_{eq}CO_2$ = equivalent emission of total greenhouse gases, where the emissions of greenhouse gases other than CO_2—e.g., methane (CH_4) and nitrous oxide (N_2O)—are converted to equivalent CO_2 emission on the basis of their impact on the greenhouse effect). These promising results show that merely reducing the need for transportation of the produce effected a significant reduction in CO_2 emissions. Yet CO_2 emissions can be further reduced by implementing rainwater harvesting practices and by using water collected from air conditioners, by conserving water applied to crops via the use of ground covers, and by using compost prepared from kitchen and garden waste rather than using industrial fertilizers, whose decomposition results in the release of nitrous oxide gases, which are powerful greenhouse gases. Indeed, the resulting carbon footprint in such a scenario may even be negative, as plant photosynthesis during vegetable growth consumes CO_2.

Environmentally Extended Input-Output Analysis (EEIOA)

An environmentally extended input-output analysis (EEIOA) entails a simple and robust method for evaluating the links between economic consumption activities and environmental impacts (Kitzes 2013). While LCA is a bottom-up process-based approach that is highly specific and that accounts mainly for the direct utilization of resources, EEIOA is a top-down methodology, and its calculation also considers the impacts of indirect contributions (Skudder et al. 2016). As such, EEIOA overcomes the limitations imposed on LCA by boundary cutoff problems (Wiedmann and Barrett 2011).

The EEIOA is ideally suited to assessing the share of services (e.g., city services) in the overall input-output analysis of a process that has multiple purposes (e.g., manufacturing, agriculture, etc.). For instance, Skudder et al. (2016) recently used the EEIOA methodology to assess the environmental impact of crime in terms of its carbon footprint. The choice of this methodology to analyze the carbon footprint of crime was motivated by the researchers' identification of an assortment of embedded emissions associated with crime. Also known as indirect emissions, they originate from the carbon associated with replacing stolen/damaged goods to that used by supporting services, such as insurance, health, legal, police, and prisons. They found that while the share of the footprint represented by stolen goods was the highest (up to 35 percent), it was followed by that of supporting services, such as health services (up to 17 percent), police activity (10 percent), prison services (8 percent), defensive expenditures (10 percent), and lastly, insurance (4 percent). Together these separate contributions to the carbon footprint constituted up to 50 percent of the greenhouse gas emissions associated with crime.

City Metabolism

To quantify material and energy flow and utilization and to control their operations and manage their services, cities around the world regularly measure a variety of indexes. Additionally, cities also perform different resource-based surveys, such as measuring the greenhouse gas emissions from different municipal sectors, to assess the impact of the city's daily life on its citizens and surroundings. These monitoring efforts provide the data necessary to design and implement the tools and actions required to address what is perhaps the most undesirable consequence of urbanization—excessive greenhouse gas emissions associated with contemporary human lifestyles. Toward that end, the collection and analysis of the material and energy flow data of a city can facilitate more rational decision making by city stakeholders to ensure that the city remains healthy and livable for its future generations.

One of the models used to calculate city-level resource flow and to provide the notion of city sustainability with practical meaning is the metabolism model (i.e., urban metabolism). Conceptually similar to human metabolism, the city metabolism model measures the rate of resource consumption and the corresponding amounts of waste generated in a certain area (e.g., city) and translates it into carbon, water, and ecological footprints. In the frame of the metabolism model, city sustainability is assessed by measuring the total energy and materials that flow into the urban area (e.g., water, food, fuel, clothing, etc.) and the total emissions that flow out of it (e.g., air pollution, sewage, and solid waste) (Kennedy, Pincetl, and Bunje 2011).

In 2014, the city of Beer-Sheva, Israel, measured and inventoried its greenhouse gas emissions over a 13-year period from 2000 to 2012 as part of its membership obligations to ICLEI-Local Governments for Sustainability, a leading global network of more than 1,500 cities, towns,

Table 3.1 Greenhouse gas emissions in Beer-Sheva

Sector	2000		2008		2012	
	eqCO$_2$	Share (%)	eqCO$_2$	Share (%)	eqCO$_2$	Share (%)
Municipal	37,322	4	44,823	5	52,691	5
Domestic	230,126	27	282,007	30	327,710	30
Commercial	207,388	24	233,392	25	374,063	34
Industry	67,321	8	84,190	9	106,041	10
Transportation	120,013	14	148,439	16	122,350	11
Waste	204,387	24	135,748	15	121,033	11
Total	865,707	100	928,600	100	1,103,887	100

and regions committed to building a sustainable future. The public-sector data for Beer-Sheva (e.g., energy and water consumption, waste and recycling, landscaping, and more) were retrieved from municipal environmental data, while the residents' data, for both homes and businesses, were provided by the electric and water companies. The emissions from the different city sectors in 2000, 2008, and 2012 are summarized in Table 3.1.

The results of the survey show that between 2000 and 2012, overall city emissions increased by 27 percent, a rate similar to that of the city's population growth during the same period. Additionally, the findings show that emissions connected with the domestic and commercial sectors not only increased steadily during that period, they consistently accounted for more than half of the city's total emissions. The municipal sector, on the other hand, was found to be directly responsible for only about 5 percent of overall city emissions, the main contributing sources to which were water and sanitation, street lighting, and public buildings (Table 3.2). The data also show that the relative share of emissions from the waste sector decreased by more than 40 percent between 2000 and 2012, a finding that is a direct result of the city's implementation of a new waste recycling program. By diverting city waste from the landfills, this program effectively reduced greenhouse gas emissions per ton of treated waste. However, the concomitant doubling of the level of trade in Beer-Sheva during the same period resulted in a 80 percent increase

Table 3.2 Greenhouse gas emissions for the municipal sector in
Beer-Sheva

	Energy consumption (Mega kWh)	Share (%)	eqCO$_2$ (kilotons)
Street and traffic lights	20.5	34	16.2
Public buildings	14.3	24	11.3
Water and sewage	25.7	42	20.3

Table 3.3 Examples of projects that contributed to reduction in
Beer-Sheva's greenhouse gas emissions

Sector	Action	Investment ($10^3/ year)*	Savings ($10^3/ year)	Emission reduction (tons eqCO$_2$)	Equivalent savings from emission reductions ($10^3/ year)**
Waste	Recycling	100	58	3,260	82
Energy efficiency	Replacement of lightbulbs in the city space	26	185	1,249	31
Garden-ing	Tree plant-ing	35	-----	1,050	26
Total		161	243	5,599	139

*Based on 10 years in total
**$25 per kg eqCO$_2$

in greenhouse gas emissions share associated with the commercial sector,
which includes retail stores and offices.

Finally, to further reduce its emissions, the city also invested in
technologies. One such technology, the computerization of the municipal irrigation system, led to an immediate and significant reduction in
municipal water consumption. Insofar as supplying a city's water needs
relies on energy—to desalinate sea water or to pump water from wells
and to transfer the water to its point of use—the computerization of the
city's irrigation system reduced the greenhouse gas emissions associated
with these activities (Table 3.3). For these currently minor achievements
to have significant and long-term impacts, however, the goal of reducing

greenhouse gas emissions must include both domestic and commercial sectors. The main challenge, therefore, is to instill in every house and business the common desire to cut emissions. To that end, the municipality is ideally situated to disseminate the message by implementing different services, from education programs and advertising to dedicated programs that help retail businesses make their operations greener.

Based on the survey and on the city's ability to design, manage, and invest in projects that could contribute to the reduction of its greenhouse gas emissions, a list of potential projects was suggested (Table 3.4). The final decisions regarding which projects would be included in the program were taken using a prioritization model built in the framework of the city's master plan for the reduction of its carbon footprint. To that end, each project was assessed on the basis of five criteria: (1) costs and resources, (2) reduction potential, (3) the potential to implement the

Table 3.4 *Prioritization of proposed projects to reduce greenhouse gases in Beer-Sheva*

No.	Project	Ranking
1	Gardening and tree planting	3.80
2	Waste management	3.70
3	Green building in new construction	3.60
4	Installation of solar panels on roofs of municipal buildings	3.30
5	Energy efficiency measures: replacement of inefficient electrical equipment (e.g., air conditioners)	3.30
6	Education for children	3.30
7	Energy savings in the commercial sector	3.15
8	Sustainable transportation master plan	3.05
9	Energy efficiency measures: replacement of conventional street lighting	3.05
10	Energy efficiency measures: streamlining municipal institutions	3.00
11	Education for adults	2.60
12	Energy efficiency measures: wastewater treatment	2.50
13	Publicity	2.20
14	Green building in the renovation of old buildings	1.50
15	Community gardens	1.20

project immediately, (4) the complexity of the process in terms of the participating entities, and (5) degree of visibility and impact of the project on changes in the city. Each project was then prioritized on a scale of 1 (low priority) to 5 (high priority).

Prioritization analysis

1. Gardening and tree planting, waste management, and the implementation of green building principles in new buildings are all top-priority activities. Already being actively promoted in the city, these projects have high greenhouse gas reduction potential and they will drive highly visible changes in the urban environment. The analysis thus led to the recommendation that these projects be given the highest priority and that they be implemented in the first stage of any municipally driven efforts to improve the city's carbon footprint.

2. The installation of photovoltaic panels on the roofs of schools is currently ongoing. Since the municipality leases schools' roof space to solar companies, the city does not incur a monetary cost in realizing the project. Though the project's emissions reduction potential is relatively low, it is simple to implement and is highly visible.

3. The replacement of inefficient electrical equipment with newer, more efficient alternatives is a relatively small project, but it is comparatively cheap and its reduction potential is high.

4. The youth education project received a high ranking because it is easy to implement and inexpensive, it affects the broader population, and it has a significant positive impact on the city. However, its emissions reduction potential is immeasurable.

5. A master plan for sustainable transportation was ranked eighth due to the high estimated cost for its implementation. Despite its high initial costs and corresponding low-priority ranking, however, the sustainable transport project was strongly recommended for immediate implementation, as it will affect all residents of the city as well as visitors, and it will help raise awareness of urban sustainability among city residents.

6. The implementation of energy efficiency measures in street lighting and in municipal institutions not only is easy, it also has a relatively high emission reduction potential. Due to the relatively high initial

investment required to implement such changes, however, they are ranked ninth and tenth in the prioritization scheme. Nevertheless, the exchange of conventional street lighting with today's more efficient alternatives was recommended for immediate implementation on new streets to demonstrate the commitment of the municipality to reducing the city's carbon footprint.

7. The renovation of buildings according to green building principles received a relatively low ranking due to the difficulties inherent in its implementation, as it requires the intimate collaboration of city residents, and due to its relatively high costs. Moreover, its emissions reduction potential is unknown.

Nonphysical Resource Measures

The quantification of the nonphysical resources—such as time, effort, or knowledge—involved in a process or service and along the value chain is much more difficult. Insofar as services provide intangible value, the nonphysical measure assessed for a service is performance, which is evaluated in terms of productivity, efficiency, and quality. Stated differently, a service's performance is reflected in its organization, level of customer satisfaction, the extent to which mutual trust develops between provider and customer, and the profits generated by the service (Rust and Oliver 1994; Johnston and Jones 2004; Wolfson et al. 2015).

A time assessment, a classic example of nonphysical resource quantification, is a potentially valuable tool whose resultant data can be practically applied toward improving the process and increasing customer satisfaction as well as the service's sustainability. In addition, time assessments can yield information that can promote the efficient allocation of the provider's resources, from the amount of manpower required to complete a given assignment to the qualifications of the employees doing the work, the amount of computing time needed, and the choice of computer software. Indeed, the mismanagement of these and other provider resources can lead to higher overall costs to the provider (i.e., life cycle costs).

The assessment of another nonphysical resource, effort, that was invested by the provider and the customer in the cocreation of a service, can also help identify more efficient routes to perform the service, and thus to increase the sustainability of a solution. For instance, the decision to participate in organized carpooling (i.e., more passengers per journey) instead of driving alone will require greater effort on the part of all stakeholders—the driver and passengers—to coordinate the logistical details. However, assuming that each carpool passenger represents one less car on the road, their carpooling efforts will also reduce their respective environmental footprint, as the resources that were allocated for the journey before carpooling (i.e., more cars making the same trip) are now split between all the passengers traveling in a single vehicle.

Another important nonphysical measure for evaluating services is the level of the value created by the service, and in general, the higher that value, the better the service. The quality of the value can be assessed by using the data/information/knowledge/intelligence/wisdom (DIKIW) pyramid or hierarchy, which ranks the overall value of a service in terms of where it is situated on the DIKIW pyramid (Ackoff 1989). In this respect, the creation of wise values begins with the collection of raw data that is communicated and then processed into information that can eventually be utilized to inform decision making and generate more knowledge. This knowledge can then be invested in intelligent solutions that increase process efficiency and that ultimately generate wisdom that increases the effectiveness of the value. In short, a wise value is that which strikes a balance between individual and collective human values while having a positive impact on future generations (Spohrer et al. 2016; Wolfson 2016).

In terms of the sustainability of a city, municipal services create a range of values that can be assessed using the DIKIW hierarchy. For example, reports about the number of complaints citizens submitted to the city by telephone or e-mail or the amount of garbage that was collected per month constitute typical crude municipal *data*. Insofar as such crude data typically provide only a general picture of what happens in the city, they usually are insufficient by themselves to form a basis for action. Yet the city can publish *information* about city events, such as the type, time, and place of the event, which allows both the city's inhabitants and its visitors to not only know what is happening in the city, but also enables them to plan their schedules and activities accordingly, regardless of whether they choose to participate in the event. Likewise, municipal services also provide citizens with *knowledge* that, as a value, allows them to reap more benefits from the service, thereby performing more complex action—for instance, giving citizens insight and assistance regarding the city's laws and procedures while he submit a building program. With respect to *intelligence* as a value, it should be an integration of data, information, and knowledge from different fields. It could be contained, for example, in the preparation of a master plan in a certain field or of a municipal budget. However, strategic plans must consider myriad future requirements that transcend current needs and wants while integrating numerous factors and including uncertainties and forecasting to yield a smart value.

Finally, assessments of the level of the value of every service, and even of the building blocks of each service's value chain, can increase the value and improve the service, ultimately to achieve higher customer satisfaction. For example, a call center or comparable Internet-based platform that allows citizens or other stakeholders to submit complaints and queries is usually situated at the level of data or, at the most, information. However, the inclusion of a built-in questionnaire may enable the service to collect more accurate and valuable information that may even qualify as knowledge. For example, a citizen report about a potentially dangerous event in the city (e.g., flooded bridge, traffic accident) can provide data about the event's location and time (i.e., information), but it could also include personal details about the person who submitted the report and whether this was an isolated event or something that occurs periodically (i.e., knowledge). Moreover, more intelligent value can be gained from the report submittal service by rapidly addressing the issue in the report (i.e., the dangerous event) and then reporting back to the complainant about what was done, which would also encourage their continued use of the service. The extent to which the municipality responds in a timely manner, as well as the effectivity of its response, is a significant contributor to the value of the service. Furthermore, the integration of the data and information obtained from the complaint and from the actions that were taken and their subsequent incorporation in municipal action plans can increase the level of the value to wisdom.

Another service offered in many cities today that can be analyzed in terms of its value and the extent to which it promotes city sustainability is that of recycling. The data and information about the placement and emptying times of collection bins and about the average amounts of recycled material collected over a given time period (e.g., per day/month/year) can be combined with information about the recyclable materials. Thus, information about the path taken by the recyclable materials, from their production in a factory to the city where they are consumed to the recycling plant, and about the subsequent uses of the recycled product can be illustrated on the product container, on the city's collection bins, and/or on the municipal website. The collection and processing of such data provides stakeholders with important knowledge about the manufacturing process from which the product is obtained and the consequences of this process. Applied to the example of a plastic bottle, the intelligent knowledge provided vis-à-vis the city's recycling endeavor can be leveraged—via supporting services such as advertising and educational programs—to motivate people to make smarter choices when shopping in the supermarket. In the long term, as more people become aware of the deleterious effects of plastic on their environment, this particular combination of services could lead to lower plastic bottle production levels and the accumulation of correspondingly less waste.

City Performance Measures

All of the cities worldwide measure different indicators and indexes. Recently, the International Organization for Standardization (ISO) issued standards—named indicators for city services and quality of life (ISO 2014)—for the sustainable development of communities. Representative examples of these indicators are listed in Table 3.5.

Table 3.5 Representative city performance measures

Topic	Indicator
Education	Percentage of students that complete secondary education
Economy	Percentage of city population that lives in poverty
Water and Sanitation	Total domestic water consumption per capita (liters/day)
Wastewater	Percentage of the city's wastewater that undergoes tertiary treatment
Solid waste	Percentage of city's solid waste that is recycled
Energy	Total residential electrical use per capita (kWh/year)
Environment	Greenhouse gas emissions measured in tons per capita
Transportation	Annual number of public transport trips per capita
Governance	Women as a percentage of the total number of elected city officials
Telecommunication and Innovation	Number of cellphones per 100,000 people in the population

The indicators in Table 3.5 are designed not only to keep the public informed by providing metrics data related to long-term community legacy goals, but also to promote the city's goals and objectives. In addition, these measures can be used as objective tools, specific to each city department, to evaluate the quality and efficiency of work.

Most cities also measure success parameters via assessments of the efficiency of their performance or of the residents' levels of satisfaction with city services, which is usually done through dedicated questionnaires and surveys that measure performance (Andreassen 1994; Kantorová and Růžička 2015). Done regularly, such assessments can indicate how effectively and efficiently the city delivers its services, and the knowledge the city obtains can then be applied to continuously improve those services and to guide the city in its subsequent planning efforts. For example, the city of Novato, California, surveyed its residents for their opinions about the community and about the quality of the services provided by the local government. A representative sample of 3,000 households was surveyed with a 28 percent response rate and a 3 percent margin of error (City of Novato 2013). Table 3.6 illustrates some representative results in different fields. To ensure that such assessments provide reliable and useful data, however, the assessment process itself must be evaluated. For example, police department of the city of Dallas submitted an audit of its performance measurement process that included five selected performance measures. The audit showed that results reported for only two of the five performance measures were reliable (City of Dallas 2016).

Table 3.6 Representative results of city of Novato citizen survey

Field	Service	Excellent rating (%)	Good rating (%)	Benchmark*
Transportation	Street repair	8	32	Similar
	Sidewalk maintenance	8	39	Much lower
	Bus or transit services	13	43	Lower
Housing	Availability of affordable quality housing	8	34	Much higher

Land use and zoning	Animal control	16	55	Similar
Community sustainability	Employment opportunities	4	23	Much lower
	Shopping opportunities	14	29	Lower
Environmental sustainability	Cleanliness	14	58	Much lower
	Quality of overall natural environment	29	55	Much higher
Culture, arts, and education	Educational opportunities	9	43	Much lower
Health and Wellness	Availability of affordable quality food	20	51	Similar

* Comparison to California cities with populations of 32,000 to 65,000.

Social Life Cycle Assessment (S-LCA)

An S-LCA comprises a set of methods used to assess the potential or real social impacts of a product or service. The term "social impacts" as used here refers to human capital, human well-being, cultural heritage, and social behavior (Jørgensen 2008; Muthu 2015). The overall goal of performing an S-LCA is to improve the social performance of products at different stages of their life cycles while considering the relevant stakeholders in their entirety (e.g., workers, customers, local community, and the city) (Wu, Yang, and Chen 2014). An S-LCA can be applied via two main routes: (1) by focusing on a performance reference point, such as workers' living and working conditions (e.g., human rights, labor conditions, and discrimination), and (2) by focusing on impact pathways, which here relate to humans and their biological living conditions (e.g., health and safety).

For example, solid-waste management services in Kathmandu, Nepal, were assessed with an S-LCA (Gautam 2011). The stakeholders of the evaluation were identified as workers, the local community, society, and all actors in the value chain. Representative indicators that were assessed during the study and the main findings are illustrated in Table 3.7.

Table 3.7 S-LCA of solid-waste management services in Kathmandu, Nepal (Gautam 2011)

Indicator	Findings
Income source and fair salary	Waste pickers earn from Rs. 15,000 to Rs. 22,500 (approx. $145 to $220), which is above the regular minimum salary of a government employee.
Working hours	Formal waste workers: two shifts of six hours each. Informal waste workers: no fixed hours and their earnings are linked to the amounts of recyclables they collect (to collect more, they must work longer hours).
Women and children	A large proportion of waste workers, particularly among street and dump pickers, were observed to be women and children.
Health and safety	Despite their vulnerability to infectious diseases, waste workers lack direct health support from the relevant authority.

Sustainable Service Assessment

To ensure the sustainability of a service in general and that of a city's agglomeration of services in particular, each service should be considered in terms of its environmental, social, and economic impacts via a sustainable service assessment. Moreover, the service should be assessed in terms of all activities and inputs and outputs associated with the service (i.e., life cycle assessment), and its value chain should be illustrated in terms of all the physical and nonphysical resources utilized in each building block of the chain. The resources should then be quantified—if possible, for each link in the value chain, but if not, then for the entire value chain—to promote improved resource allocation and to design more efficient and effective services. In addition, as the production and delivery of a service necessitate the involvement of both the provider and the customer, the division in resources between the two should also be presented. Likewise, the distribution between the resources associated with the core-value (CV) of the service (i.e., the essence of the solution that a certain service provides) and those associated with the super-value (SV) (i.e., other supporting and complementary values) should also be considered. Finally, as the same service can be provided via different modes (e.g., electronic service, self-service, etc.), LCA should be done for each mode in a manner that facilitates their comparison to enable people to choose intelligently between them.

To illustrate a sustainable service assessment, the payment process for municipal services was chosen. The assessment was done in terms of direct physical resources (e.g., water, energy), facilities (e.g., office, computer), effort (e.g., time and manpower), and the value according to the DIKIW pyramid (Ackoff 1989).

Cities provide different methods of payment for municipal services such as education, document issuing, and refuse collection. Traditionally, municipal services were paid for in the person-to-person (P2P) mode in the relevant city office, at the bank, or at the post office. Today such payments can be made via a phone call, on the city's website, or by using different smartphone applications. For example, most cities today offer an e-service that allows customers to remotely pay for municipal services online instead of driving to the municipal office or the bank to make the transaction through a teller. Table 3.8 illustrates the division of resources and capabilities between provider and customer in the P2P and e-service modes in terms of the service's CV and SV.

Table 3.8 Comparison of the division of resources and capabilities between customer and provider in person-to-person (P2P) and e-service payment modes

	Value	1. P2P		2. e-service	
		Provider	Consumer	Provider	Customer
Resources	CV	Paper, electricity	None	Electricity	Electricity
	SV	Electricity, water, etc.	Gasoline	Electricity, water, etc.	None
Facilities	CV	Office, computer	None	Website, computer	Computer/ mobile phone
	SV	Building, server farm	Car or bus, etc.	Server farm	Home/office
Effort	CV	Manpower	None	Manpower	Internet use
	SV	Office and building operation	Driving to the city hall/ bank; standing in line; car or bus operation	Office operation	None

(Continued)

Table 3.8 (Continued)

	Value	1. P2P		2. e-service	
		Provider	**Consumer**	**Provider**	**Customer**
Knowledge	CV	Payment system operation	None	Payment system operation	Internet use
	SV	Office and building operation	Car or bus operation	Server farm and system operation	No
Carbon footprint [(gCO₂)—total]		421–1519[1]		127–307[2]	

[1] On the basis of carbon footprint measurements for various transportation means per passenger-kilometer-traveled (Chester and Arpad 2009) and carbon footprint measurement per employee by HomeStreet Bank (Seattle Climate Partnership 2009).
[2] On the basis of transaction times of 10 minutes (Google Environmental Report 2017).

Both payment scenarios could be made more sustainable by using more efficient technologies—for example, by using electricity that is based on renewable energy (e.g., solar or wind power) or by using conventionally produced electricity more efficiently (e.g., more efficient computers). Not only can these solutions save money, they can also result in the generation of less pollution. But, as illustrated in Table 3.8, shifting from a P2P service to an e-service affects all aspects of the service in terms of both the CV and the SV provided by each service. Regarding physical resources and facilities, while the P2P mode requires a building and an office, which require a multitude of resources for their daily operation, from water and electricity to paper, computers, and furniture, the e-service mode requires neither an office nor a building, and it eliminates the need for the customer's transportation to and from the office. Moreover, the e-service also requires less manpower. Yet the shift to a reliance on e-services requires greater customer involvement in terms of resources and capabilities, as the customers, who perform the bulk of the activity, must use their own facilities (e.g., home, computer, and Internet line) and invest their effort and knowledge. However, the time that the customer must invest and the total energy used per transaction are also lower in the e-service mode. Furthermore, the physical resources associated with each service's SV are tremendously different between the two modes. For one, making the shift to the e-services mode renders the office and the corresponding resources required for its operation (but that are not directly needed or involved in the payment itself) redundant. This finding is in agreement with similar results showing that a significant reduction in resources can be achieved by shifting from the super-service mode (i.e., service is operated mainly by the provider) to the self-service mode (i.e., service is operated mainly by the customer) of a given service (Wolfson, Tavor, and Mark 2012).

The next step of the assessment should be the division of resources between the various stages of the life cycle. The value chains of the P2P and e-service service modes are illustrated in Figure 3.1. Two representative analyses were performed to compare the two scenarios: (1) physical resources in terms of greenhouse gas emissions and (2) nonphysical resources in terms of time.

The total greenhouse gas emissions of the P2P mode of a bill payment service comprised two main components: the energy used (by both provider and customer) to travel to and from the municipal office or bank and the energy used by the provider to maintain the office. The greenhouse gas emissions of a journey depend on the type of vehicle and on the roundtrip distance traveled to the municipal office or bank. Chester and Arpad (2009) performed an environmental assessment of passenger transportation based on energy use or greenhouse gas emissions per passenger-kilometer-traveled (PKT). The survey included operational components that can be assigned to the service's CV (e.g., running the vehicle and idling time) and nonoperational components that can be assigned to the service's SV (e.g., vehicle manufacture, maintenance and insurance,

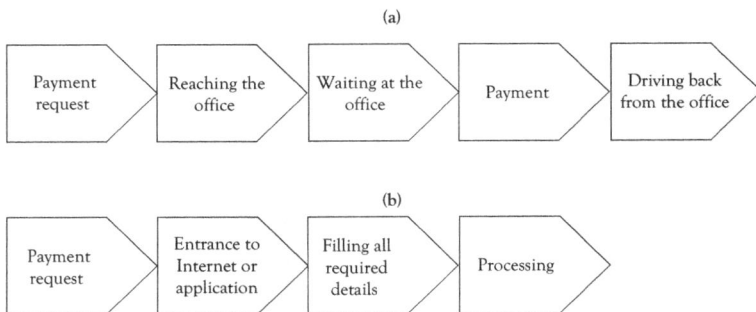

Figure 3.1 Value chain of payment for municipal service: (a) P2P, (b) e-service

infrastructure construction, operation and maintenance, and fuel production). They found emissions of 51 gCO_2 PKT in the case of an urban
diesel bus at peak hours and 234 gCO_2 PKT for a car with one passenger.
Thus, as expected, using public transport in the P2P service mode is much
more sustainable than using private transport. Considering a round-trip
journey of 6 km, the total emission of the customer is between 306 and
1,404 gCO_2. To this should be added the emissions of the provider.
HomeStreet Bank calculated greenhouse gas emissions per employee for
a year (Seattle Climate Partnership 2009), assuming 25 working days per
month and 10-hour workdays and considering employee commuting,
energy use, waste generation, and so on. Based on this calculation and
a scenario of 5 minutes for each transaction, the total greenhouse gas
emission is 115 gCO_2. Hence, the total emission of the P2P scenario is
between 421 and 1,519 gCO_2 and is attributed mainly to the customer.

In contrast, greenhouse gas emissions of the e-service scenario are
attributed mainly to the energy used to power the computers of the customers and those of the provider, including the provider's server farm.
In this case, the calculation was based on annual CO_2 emissions of 300
million tons generated by 1.9 billion Internet users for 365 days per year.
Each payment transaction was estimated at 10 minutes, as the customer
usually needs more time than the teller to complete the transaction, for
a total time of 10 hours of computer use. Based on this calculation, the
customer's emission is 7.3 gCO_2 while that of the provider is due mainly
to the energy used in running the server farm. To assess the emissions
of a typical server farm, Google performed a greenhouse gas emissions
analysis. Depending on the source of the energy used to power the server
farm, its emission amounted to 0.2 to 0.5 gCO_2 for each Internet search
of a duration of several seconds (Google environmental report 2017).
Therefore, the server emission generated in a 10-minute transaction is
estimated at 120 to 300 gCO_2. Taken together with the emission assigned
to the customer, the total emission for a single payment transaction is 127
to 307 gCO_2, which is attributed mainly to the provider. This greenhouse
gas emissions analysis shows clearly that exchanging the P2P service mode
with an e-service payment system results in a significant reduction in the
associated emissions.

A time assessment of the two scenarios shows that the payment process is much more efficient in the e-service mode, which can be performed at any time of day and from any location. Use of the P2P mode requires the customer to drive to and from the office, and total travel time can be estimated at 12.2 minutes (6 km roundtrip at 50 km per hour with 5 minutes allotted for parking). Add to that an average waiting time of 15 minutes before the customer is served and 5 minutes for making the actual payment through the teller, and the total time needed to pay a municipal bill in the P2P payment mode is 32.2 minutes. Performed in the e-service mode, in contrast, the whole process is estimated to take about 10 minutes. Moreover, because use of the e-service requires greater involvement in and responsibility for the process on the part of the customer, he or she can further streamline the payment process for municipal bills by making several payments each time he or she goes online to pay municipal bills. Likewise, customers can even manage their payments to the city more efficiently by, for example, making all their payments through a single application that, in addition to keeping a central record of all customer payments, can alert the customer in the event that an unusual payment is made, thereby conferring on the customer greater control over the payment process. Taken together, the many benefits of using the e-service increase the level of the value generated by the service.

Although the e-service mode is more accessible, viable, and effective in comparison with the P2P service mode, the latter should not be eliminated entirely. Because the technological solution may not be used or easily accessible by all of the citizens (e.g., the elderly, people without a computer), the municipality should continue to offer the P2P mode as a payment option. However, that could be done using a less intensive format—for example, by reducing the number of hours the payments office is open for business.

Finally, to further increase process efficiency and effectivity, its value chain can be assessed in terms of the DIKIW value hierarchy. An examination of the value chain of an e-payment system to enable citizens to pay for municipal services (Figure 3.1b) shows that the first step, the payment request, is at the level of data, the second and third steps require more knowledge, and the final step, processing, is more at the level of intelligence. Yet the location of the service as a whole in the DIKIW hierarchy can be improved through a variety of means. For instance, the first step may include information about the payment process, the essence of the payment, and how it can be reduced, which will supply the service's customers with more information or knowledge that they can then employ toward using the municipal service more efficiently in the future. Furthermore, extra steps can be added to the payment process after the final step of processing. For example, the municipality could also include an optional questionnaire to obtain customer feedback about the process that can be practically applied to improve the process itself, thus yielding a more intelligent or wise value for subsequent customers who use the e-payment service.

CHAPTER 4

Cyclicality in the City

We typically view human life as a linear process that progresses stepwise and that hopefully also includes elements of growth and advancement. For example, we invest our resources and effort early in life, such as in the pursuit of an academic degree, to harvest the anticipated benefits later in life, such as good jobs. In so doing, most of us are continuously looking ahead and moving in one direction toward the future. Even human cognitive processes, in which a response to a step is elicited before another step is taken, are usually linear. In addition, although our lives are in a sense dictated by cycles, such as the day/night cycle and the seasons of the year, perhaps because time proceeds irreversibly along a continuum, our view of time is also linear. Is this adherence to the notion of linearity the result of our understanding of the finiteness of human life and our observation of the changes our physical and mental processes undergo over time? Alternatively, perhaps it is the result of the scientific and technological advances that yield so-called progress in the form of social and economic improvement (i.e., Idea of Progress) (Bury 1987).

As illustrated by the natural cycles that drive all life on our planet, nature works in a cyclical manner. Most fundamental natural processes are performed in cycles that comprise the transformation of energy, elements (e.g., carbon or oxygen), molecules like water, and more complex matter such as nutrients in ecosystems. Likewise, many physiological systems, such as the cardiovascular and respiratory systems, also work in cyclical fashion, as do astronomical and climate cycles, which, in turn, determine agricultural cycles. The reason for the circularity of nature is that insofar as the earth is a closed system, in which matter is neither created nor destroyed, its continued functioning is dependent on cyclical processes that promote the sustainable use of physical resources for maximal efficiency. Cyclical processes also allow values to be transformed while controlling and regulating the overall process, which comprises myriad subprocesses all functioning together.

From the perspective of utilization of physical resources, to reach the ultimate goal of sustainability, manmade processes should mimic natural processes, and in so doing, they should adopt and implement the rationality of cyclical processes (e.g., renewability and recycling). Likewise, nonphysical resources (e.g., time or knowledge) should also be utilized in a cyclical manner, not only to streamline processes and conserve resources, but also to foster the renewal of those resources and even to increase their amounts. The cyclical use of knowledge—such as occurs in scientific research, for example—generates more knowledge. However, because human society has been formed largely on the basis of the goods-dominant logic, the concept of value chain (and the corresponding creation of value), which is defined as a set of activities performed in series to create and deliver value in terms of goods or services (Porter 1985), was formulated from a linear perspective. Insofar as it is fundamental to process organization, it should also be revised and redesigned to reflect cyclicality.

Circular Economy

In today's economy, natural resources are mined and extracted, turned into products, and then used, after which they are eventually discarded. This linear process depletes the natural-resource pool on the one hand and emits undesirable and even harmful and hazardous materials to the environment on the other. Moreover, with the world's population and corresponding per capita consumption increasing constantly, this linear economic model, which is based on the three steps of "take, make, and dispose," is no longer suitable. Indeed, the potential consequences of perpetuating this way of life on the natural and social environments are severe.

Instead of a linear model, a cyclic economic paradigm (i.e., circular economy) that mimics nature is needed, in which the materials and energy loops are closed (Andersen 2007). The conceptualization of the circular economy began as part of a project to find nature-mimicry technologies that could positively affect the economies of the world via the sustainable provision of basic human needs (Pauli 2010). Stahel (2014) proposed five guiding principles of the circular economy: (1) the smaller the loop (activity-wise and geographically), the more profitable and resource efficient it is; (2) loops have no beginning and no end, and "value maintained" replaces "value added"; (3) the speed of the circular flows is crucial—the efficiency of managing stock in the circular economy increases with decreasing flow speed; (4) continued ownership—through reliance on the reuse, repair, and remanufacture paradigm—without a change in ownership could halve transaction costs; and (5) a circular economy must entail functioning markets.

However, the circular economy model seeks not only to promote closed-loop production patterns by reusing and recycling resources and to streamline resource use to achieve a better balance between economy, environment, and society (Andersen 2007; Ghisellini, Cialani, and Ulgiati 2016); it also strives to improve resource conservation and renewal outcomes. Thus, it aims to change not only how resources flow in processes, but also the processes themselves. In so doing, the circular economy paradigm offers a restorative model according to which renewable resources are exploited to reduce the environmental impacts of goods production. In addition, it suggests that every economic activity be designed such that the protection of nature and ecosystems is among its principal goals. Furthermore, it has strategic and operational benefits at both the micro and the macro levels, and it will unrecognizably change the very essence of how we consume, produce, and use products, in the process altering our way of living. Finally, the vision of the circular economy closely resembles that of the *blue economy*, which dictates that we supply the basic needs of all with what we have, in the process shifting society from a state of scarcity to one of abundance.

Closed-loop product life cycles designed to confer numerous benefits on the environment, society, and the economy have already been implemented by a variety of different legal bodies, from the European Union to cities around the world. Integral to such efforts are waste management projects, from waste collection and sorting for reuse and recycling to sharing goods (European Commission 2014). Although the primary focus remains reducing the rate of waste generation and the amount of refuse that eventually reaches landfills, nascent efforts to implement fundamental changes in the design and use of products and to imbue other fields (e.g., energy production and use) with circularity are evident. In addition, the circular economy model has been perceived by most developed countries as an important and necessary part of sustainable development. Consequently, a growing number of scholars, entrepreneurs, and government officials are studying and evaluating circular economy theories, and their efforts are yielding increasingly diverse and mature applications of the model (Qian and Wang 2016).

A general example of the use of the circular economy concept that yields economic, social, and environmental benefits comprises district energy systems. Defined as centralized and combined systems for the heating, cooling, thermal storage, and other energy needs of a defined area, district energy systems improve energy management, increase supply efficiency, and enable the greater use of renewables. Moreover, this type of system is built on matching local energy production with use at the neighborhood and city levels and not merely on exploiting surplus heat or energy supplies at the building level. It thus reduces carbon emissions and increases city resilience (Su et al. 2013).

New Economic Models

Under the umbrella of the circular economy paradigm, a wide variety of other new economic models geared toward the sustainable use of physical resources—such as *green growth, local economy,* and *share economy (shareconomy)*—have attracted increased attention in recent years. Green growth refers to a scheme that broadens stakeholder opportunities and possibilities and that generates economic development and growth while sustainably using natural resources and ensuring people's well-being (Reilly 2012). The overriding objective of green growth is to decouple economic growth from increased resource use and production. Likewise, local economy is a paradigm that links the economy with community, particularly in terms of the production and consumption activities in a certain geographic area, with the goal of increasing people's prosperity by coupling the local social and natural environments (Benington 1986). Based on buying local, this approach ensures that more money stays in the local community, which can also lead to self-sufficiency. More so than green growth, however, the local economy relies critically on the implementation of closed-loop systems, which can not only benefit the community's entire population, they can also contribute significantly to the preservation of the region's natural environment. As such, the concept of local economy abides by Stahel's first principle of the circular economy (Stahel 2016).

A slightly different approach to cyclical economies was formulated as shareconomy. A prominent buzz word of the last decade, shareconomy entails another method of using natural resources in a more rational and circular manner while increasing opportunities for individuals, communities, and societies (Cheng 2016; Heinrichs 2013). In line with Stahel's fourth principle of circular economy (Stahel 2014), shareconomy envisions connecting individual stakeholders with each other to facilitate their direct sharing of the resources, assets, goods, and services of their economies. Ownership in such a system is replaced with access, and consumer behavior is not limited to merely searching for values to acquire and own (Wolfson 2016). In addition, shareconomy allows individuals to profit more from their assets, knowledge, and skills, but rather than the unidirectional exchange of the linear model, the shareconomy is built on dynamic, multidirectional interaction. As such, it encourages the interaction of multiple providers and customers—that is, its stakeholders, who can be providers one time, customers another time, or they can even play both roles simultaneously. In addition, the shareconomy promotes the disaggregation of physical resources and assets and favors their consumption as services, and insofar as it creates direct connections between people, fostering among them feelings of community, the shareconomy also has a strong social impact.

The environmental benefits of sharing are clear. These include reductions in the physical capital invested in new goods and the more efficient use of resources during all the use stages of goods' life cycles. Yet, although today the term shareconomy is loosely applied to a wide range of barter, cooperative, and sharing structures, in many such cases this designation is incorrect. Indeed, insofar as the shareconomy framework may promote consumption by providing goods and services that are identical to those offered in the conventional economy but at lower prices, it can also encourage the purchase of unnecessary goods at unsustainable levels, thereby generating an undesired rebound effect. This undesirable outcome can be prevented by using more advanced shareconomy platforms that engender not only the first two categories of sharing, that is, (1) the recirculation of goods by repeatedly reusing goods and (2) the exchange of services. In addition, the more advanced shareconomy models promote the realization of other categories—such as (3) the increased utilization of durable assets by using assets to their full capacity and (4) the sharing of production, which entails the sharing of space, real or virtual, to promote production instead of consumption—to yield greater savings and higher circularity of resources within a locality. For example, a food cooperative, which connects producers directly with consumers, enables the former to provide healthy, affordable, and accessible food to its customers. Ideally, food cooperatives should be implemented entirely at the local level, such that the food is grown and consumed in the same geographical area. This simple approach would eliminate the need for long-distance transportation to the point of sale and the waste of additional materials for the product packaging needed to transport the food. Furthermore, it would also ensure that less food gets discarded, as the produce would reach customers faster (rather than spend time on market shelves), and that the nutrients that were used to grow the food will be returned to nature in the same region where they originated, which could be done by composting (i.e., recycling) all organic waste and then distributing the compost to the relevant local stakeholders.

An integral part of the sustainable and smart cities paradigms, the shareconomy concept is also applicable in the city, where citizen-to-city and citizen-to-citizen initiatives can help solve city challenges. For instance, the popular services *Airbnb* and *Uber*, both built on shareconomy principles to supplement conventional city services, have partnerships with many cities. In addition, different city assets can be shared for creative and productive purposes—for example, giving these assets to local artists to be used as studios and for art shows and exhibitions.

Social Circles and Communities

The concept of the social circle, which can refer to a group of close friends or to a group of people who are socially connected, describes a critical aspect of human social life that is particularly relevant to the transformation from economies comprising individuals to those built on community. More than just a metaphor, the concept of circularity in the frame of community refers to multidirectional interactions (rather than linear or one-on-one interactions) between the community's members. These interactions comprise resource flows and the creation and provision of physical and nonphysical values that, in a community organized around the principles of circularity, ultimately remain within the group.

Broadly speaking, a community is a group of individuals that share common needs, and usually the group occupies a specifically defined geographical area. In biology or ecology, a community is an assemblage of populations of different species interacting with one another in a common place (e.g., a forest of trees and other plants), which is usually defined by the diversity of species within. From the perspective of human society, a community is a network of people with common values who have parallel interests regarding particular agendas and causes and who collaborate by sharing ideas, information, and other resources. Although traditionally communities in either the natural or human environment have been associated with defined areas or demarcated by clear geographical boundaries, in the virtual environment they are no longer restricted to particular physical areas.

Insofar as it is a congregation of myriad communities, all creating value, the city lends itself to the concept of circularity. Rather than groups of individuals that cocreate values in a static, linear, one-on-one connection with the city authority or between themselves (e.g., paying taxes, shopping in a local store), the city fosters the development of a community whose members also share values (e.g., community centers, clothing cooperatives) to produce a more dynamic and interactive human environment. Indeed, to ensure that the city space is all inclusive, many cities dedicate special services and resources to their different subcommunities (e.g., students, single parents, and lesbian, gay, bisexual, and transgender (LGBT) individuals) with the goal of addressing the needs of each group without depriving the other groups. The subcommunities themselves also create their own frameworks within which they generate and deliver tangible and intangible values in the city, with or without the coordination of city authorities, thus conferring on the city a greater capacity to supply the needs of its population.

The challenges facing cities today and those that future cities will have to address tomorrow can be effectively confronted by exploiting the social potential of communities. For instance, consumer behavior, which is strongly connected to social class and community conduct, can be altered by intervention from above, such as through taxes and subsidies. Alternatively, communities can choose collectively to bring about change in their socioeconomic environment by using socially based methods, such as education and publicity. Indeed, community action is known to be an important driver of change at the local level, from reduction in crime to the strengthening of local businesses. Communities can also influence how their local authorities plan, develop, and implement processes in the city. Thus, communities have the capacity to effect a more sustainable future for themselves through a variety of different means. From a social perspective, citizens must become more involved in, and assume greater responsibility for, promoting social equity and public health while encouraging all the community's members to participate in the process.

Cyclical Service

The rapid growth in service science research and development dictates that we reconsider how services are produced and delivered and what roles are played by the provider, the customer, and other actors in the process. Moreover, this reassessment must also take into account the economy and marketing trends and the relevant social and environmental implications. Like that of physical resources and tangible values, the flow of nonphysical resources and intangible values (i.e., services) can also be streamlined by moving from the linear to the circular model.

Over the years, service began to be characterized in the framework of the service-dominant logic, and the roles of the producer, the client, and other actors involved in the production and delivery of the value have changed accordingly (Vargo and Lush 2004). As noted previously, service was originally defined according to the value-in-exchange model as the transfer of an intangible value from a producer to a client in a linear process. The design and generation of the value, according to this model, is solely the responsibility of the producer, who invests all the physical and nonphysical resources relevant to provision of the service. Included among these resources are materials and energy, facilities, effort, and information and knowledge. The producer also delivers the value to the client, who simultaneously uses it, as expressed by the notion of service inseparability, and pays for it in exchange. The value is thus produced and delivered in two separate, sequential steps that resemble the production and delivery of goods (Figure 2.2a). In addition, both the producer and the client have distinct roles: the producer acts as a supplier that generates and distributes the value and manages the supply chain, while the client is actually a consumer. Throughout this linear process, the value flows in one direction.

Besides shifting the fundamental basis of exchange from tangible to intangible values, the service-dominant logic approach also marked a change in marketing, such that company preferences shifted from *marketing to their consumers* to *marketing with their customers*. It thus redefined value exchange in the framework of a value in-use model and focused on the value cocreation process. According to the value in-use model, a value is jointly and reciprocally created by the producer and the client. The interactions among all beneficiaries are also accounted for in this model via the integration of resources and the implementation of skills (Figure 2.2b) (Vargo, Maglio, and Akaka 2008). From the value in-use perspective, the notion of cocreation also divided the responsibilities for supplying the resources and capabilities relevant to the service between the producer and the client, and in so doing, it changed the corresponding roles played by the two sides in the production and transformation of the value. In fact, it transformed the supplier into a provider who, besides investing resources and capabilities, also provides the consumer with a platform that allows the latter to become actively involved in the value production and delivery process, thereby becoming a customer. The value cocreation process also emphasized another characteristic of service, its inconsistency, which reflects the wide variability of any service and the fact that the delivery of a service is never repeated in exactly the same way, as the provider, the customer, and the place and time of delivery change from one service instance to the next. In this scenario, however, the value is still delivered in one direction, from the provider to the customer.

Chandler and Vargo (2011) argued that to provide more specific and accurate value, the time, the place, and the requirements as well as the abilities of the relevant actors (i.e., provider, coproviders, and customer) should be integrated and synchronized. Accordingly, they offered a new model of value proposition, named *value-in-context,* which assigns more responsibility in the cocreation process to the customer, who should control the creation and delivery of the value in a given situation. Yet, though more responsibility is allocated in this type of model to the customer, who is more involved in the provision of the value, the value still flows in one direction in linear fashion. An alternative notion of value cocreation was advanced by Wolfson et al. (2010, 2015) in their sustainable services model. In their model, which depicts service as the integration of a *core-value* (the purpose and essence of the service) with a *super-value* (other supportive or complementary, intangible values associated with the service), they suggest that the provider should allow and even encourage the customer to become a coprovider of sustainability as a super-value to both the current and future generations (Figure 2.2c). In addition, the cocreation process is driven by multiple direct and indirect customers who should participate, either actively or passively, in the process. Thus, in this type of model, although the core-value flows from the provider to the customer, the super-value flows from the customer to the provider or from both of them to other customers.

The joint generation and delivery of a super-value by the customer and the provider to subsequent customers is not limited to sustainability science or social justice. Moreover, the core-value can also be regenerated from the customer to the provider, after which it can be cogenerated and delivered by both and then used by other direct customers or stakeholders (Figure 2.2c). This cogeneration process, termed value in-return, progressively recruits additional customers to the service and also transforms customers into providers (Wolfson 2016). Yet value in-return does not signify merely the assignment of another role or new tasks to the customer or the transfer of part of the value from the customer to the provider and their cogeneration of a new value to be delivered to other customers. In addition, this new paradigm dictates that as the value must be returned, the involvement of the customer as a coprovider in the cocreation and use of the original value must also change. Finally, these changes in the roles, attitudes, and skills of both the provider and the customer alter the entire value generation and delivery process, a change that may ultimately result in the generation of a value that is considerably different from the service's original value. Under the value in-return model, therefore, the cogeneration of services not only has the potential to make services more efficient and productive, it also renews some of the resources in a circular manner.

To demonstrate how the models' value chains differ from one another and the benefits of shifting from a linear to a circular model, a hotel booking service can be used as an example. In the value in-exchange model, the client, who uses an agent to reserve a room, determines the time, the location, and other requirements such as price limit and necessary room and hotel facilities, while the agent performs all searches and makes subsequent booking arrangements. In this scenario, the value (i.e., hotel reservation) flows from the supplier to the client, who pays for the service. Alternatively, hotel booking over the Internet can follow a value-in-use paradigm. Enabled by advances in information and communication technologies (ICTs), an online hotel booking service like Booking.com allows anybody to easily search for a hotel according to their specific requirements. As the service's provider, Booking.com precludes the need for a mediator (i.e., travel agent). In this value in-use model, although customers must invest more time and effort to search for the desired hotel, they eliminate the agent's commission in the deal, thus obtaining the service at a lower price. These benefits of online hotel booking enable customers to more accurately meet their requirements. In addition, the provision of the value can be done at any time and from almost any location, thereby conferring on the service an element of convenience for customers, who are not restricted to booking their hotels during travel agent working hours.

Despite the more efficient provision of value in the value-in-use scenario, however, its flow is still unidirectional, from provider to customer. To create a service with greater circularity requires that the service be designed based on the value in-return model, according to which the customer can also return value to the provider in the form of either a core- or a super-value. For example, many hotel reservation sites award hotels that are booked through their site points and then compile ratings lists, on which each hotel is ranked based on the number of times it was chosen by customers, which subsequent customers can use to gain some insight about the numbers of people who used the hotels they are considering. To return even higher value both to the provider and to subsequent customers, hotel booking sites often request feedback from their customers about the hotels they used by, for example, scoring the hotel on the booking website or filling out a questionnaire about the hotel. This feedback mechanism, which depends on the wisdom of the crowd, returns value to the provider that is cogenerated with the provider and that will also benefit all customers who use the same website. This is in fact a multiprovider and multicustomer system, in which everyone on both sides shares in the responsibility for the provision of service.

The value in-return model is highly applicable to city services, but not merely as it applies to resource efficiency. First of all, insofar as it strives to inculcate in each citizen a sense of responsibility toward the city's other members, it also generates communities. In addition, the value in-return model allows—and in fact obliges—each stakeholder to become actively involved in the services that are provided in the city. Properly applied, it can be an efficacious route to advance the value in the value hierarchy (i.e., DIKIW hierarchy (Ackoff 1989)). An everyday example of a service that reflects the value in-return model is the "civil guard" system in Israel, which comprises citizen volunteers who assist in daily police work. Initially conceived as an opportunity for citizens to combat local crime and instill in their fellow residents a feeling of security, civil guard programs are active in many cities in Israel. As the citizens are both providers and beneficiaries of the service, the Israeli civil guard system qualifies as a municipal value in-return service.

Sustainability Cycle

Considering sustainability as a service (Wolfson 2015, 2016), it can also be viewed as a value chain that can be renewed and, therefore, as a cycle. Such a cycle should integrate physical values of matter and energy with nonphysical values such as information, knowledge, awareness, and the appropriate methods while ensuring the subsequent renewal of all these resources. In other words, similar to how we portray life cycles, we can also define a *sustainability cycle*. But beyond the requirement that it imitate natural processes via the renewal and maintenance of resources, the sustainability cycle should also be driven by the notion of progress and be able to adapt to changes in the environment in evolutionary fashion.

Thus, it should refer to a process designed to receive and to reciprocate, to be a whole unto itself but also to be part of something bigger, and ultimately, to be a process that learns from the past, changes the present, and considers the future. The adoption of such a perspective can enable the sustainability cycle to yield the highest value.

The implementation of a sustainable cycle must begin with proper planning and involve innovative foresight built on the lessons of past experience. In parallel with planning, the tangible and intangible social, economic, and environmental values that are incorporated in the process and that can affect individuals as well as all of society in the short and long terms, locally and globally, should be characterized in detail. The next stage of implementing a sustainable cycle should entail the delineation of which values are related to the core-value and the super-value of the process, during which the most significant and influential values are identified. By identifying the definitive parameters of a sustainable cycle, its value can be broken down and quantified for use in comparative analyses to assess all the relevant options and to determine the stage in the cycle with the most potential to streamline the process and increase its value. Although currently no single value that can reliably display all the dimensions of sustainability exists, several established metrics can be used together to assess the overall sustainability of a cycle or process.

However, for sustainability to progress from a mere ideology or methodology to practical realization, it must have a value that can be changed, and, equally important, the extent of that change must be measureable. The economic value of the sustainability cycle should be based on savings. In the short term, these savings are reflected in the extent to which the amounts of resources used in the cycle are reduced, and in the long term, they are realized by implementing sustainable development that strives to conserve resources and reduce ecological damage. The sustainability cycle also has a clear social value, as it promotes basic human values such as fairness, community, justice, and equality, and it allows every member of the community to participate in a significant, synergistic process whose whole is much greater than its parts. The implementation of practices that promote sustainability, in turn, will make us better people who not only care about each other, but who are also invested in the upkeep of our environment, and in so doing, we will create resilient communities.

Finally, the environmental value of the sustainability cycle begins with our appreciation of the beauty and sheer power of nature and the understanding that we are collectively an integral part of natural cycles and that, as such, we must aim to coexist in harmony with the natural ecosystems that are critical to our planet's health. The adoption of this mindset will beget additional environmental value, as it will encourage us to actively protect the natural environment and allow nature to support its biotic and nonbiotic components and its ecosystems. Lastly, the knowledge that we are preserving our natural environment, thereby ensuring that it will remain intact for future generations to continue to receive ecosystem services, is also an environmental value.

Examples

Waste Management

Cities around the world are increasingly turning to the concept of circularity as the basis for viable city operational strategies that will promote the survival of the city into the future. Essential to the perpetuation of any city is its waste management scheme, which here is used to illustrate how circularity can be incorporated into a common city service.

A fundamental municipal service, waste collection refers to the transfer of solid waste from its point of inception to a treatment center or to a landfill. In the simplest sense, the service value chain of waste management comprises garbage collection by its producers, (i.e., city residents and businesses), who also help streamline the service by sorting their garbage according to assigned bins that are distributed throughout the city. The city then assumes responsibility for waste pickup and subsequent transfer to centralized treatment facilities. Yet, while conventional waste treatment typically entailed the disposal of natural resources in landfills—which today are known to be environmental hazards that pollute land, water, and air, that produce undesirable odors, and that attract pests (e.g., insects, rodents, etc.)—the service of waste collection was redesigned as the broader service of waste management.

From the perspective of a service, shifting from a strategy of waste collection to one of waste management transforms the service mode from value in-exchange to value in-use and even to value in-return. In terms of a sustainable service, the value chain of the service should be initiated by waste reduction efforts (e.g., minimization or prevention of waste generation) and the more rational use of products (e.g., using larger packages and recyclable or biodegradable packing materials). These goals can be achieved not only by adding supporting services, such as education and advertising to inform the public at large, but also by instituting a fee program that assigns a different municipal rate to each citizen based on the amount of garbage he or she produces. The supporting services that will be needed to effectively implement a waste management strategy can be facilitated by exploiting the inherent power of social circles and community in a process that can even change deeply ingrained habits.

To obtain circularity in any waste management system, the final stage in the value chain, the landfill, should be eliminated in favor of waste treatment processes that exploit the remaining material and energy by, for example, recycling the dry components, composting the wet components, and recovering energy (e.g., incineration or anaerobic digestion to biogas). The elimination of landfills requires waste sorting at the beginning of the value chain to close the cycle at the end, thus creating a value in-return system in which the value is cogenerated by the city's residents and its municipal authorities. The closure of the value chain in a cycle should include the return of at least some of the resources processed in the waste treatment system back to the city or even to its residents. For example, compost produced with the city's garbage can be used to fertilize city gardens or energy produced using city waste can be used to generate steam for heating or electricity for lighting. Moreover, composting can be performed at both the city and the community levels—on a large scale by the municipality and on a small scale by citizens—for use in community gardens. Lastly, under the sustainability circle model, the waste treatment facilities should be located in or close to the city and they should employ the citizens.

Parking Services

Parking is the simple act of halting one's vehicle and leaving it, usually temporarily, in a designated area, unoccupied, until the vehicle is needed again. The facilities that are available for parking include streets, lots, and garages, among others, some of which are free, either indefinitely or for limited times, while others rely on payment systems.

One way that parking can be utilized to facilitate the more sustainable use of city parking assets is to couple free or inexpensive parking services with public transportation, that is, the placement of parking lots near train stations or on the outskirts of the city. In addition, parking can also be shared using different mechanisms. For instance, private parking spaces can be used by other people when the owner of the parking space is not using it. This simple space-sharing mechanism can increase the parking pool of the city, in the process transforming parking customers who share their spaces into parking providers in a value in-return model to generate a cyclic service.

In the frame of the circular economy, such parking schemes can substantially reduce the number of cars on the road daily, which can lead to less congested roadways and decrease in vehicle-generated pollution levels in the city. Likewise, the use of carpooling to share car journeys, or carsharing, in which a rental car or a personal vehicle is shared for short periods of time, can also reduce the numbers of cars entering the city on a daily basis, thereby reducing the pressure on the city's parking assets. In this respect, a more sustainable solution involves the use of ICT to work, shop, or perform administrative activities remotely instead of driving into the city and occupying a city parking space.

CHAPTER 5

The Service-City Model

Cities are without a doubt one of the main channels to achieve sustainable development and economic and social growth. Yet cities are also the cause of many economic and social problems (European Union 2011). For example, while the contribution cities make to the gross domestic product (GDP) is typically very high, many cities suffer from severe unemployment and poverty, which can sap their resources and become a drain on their respective countries. Likewise, while cities typically contribute markedly to the art and other cultural assets of their respective countries—cities usually house a variety of museums, galleries, theaters, and art schools—the related cultural activities are often led by very small and close-knit groups of people and organizations, and therefore, they are not always accessible to all the city's residents and visitors. At last, although many cities in the world have taken the lead with respect to issues of environmental quality, developing and advancing many important programs and projects in the field (Portney 2005; Lehmann 2010), cities are simultaneously responsible for high share in the amount of pollution generated, due, for example, to greenhouse gas emissions and garbage production. City planning and growth efforts, therefore, should aim for greater alignment between the city's problems and their solutions.

At their most basic level, cities are also spaces of services. In fact, all city activities can be defined as the exchange of services between a wide variety of stakeholders—namely, residents, traders, visitors, and city authorities (Frug 1998; Miguel, Tavares, and Araújo 2012). Therefore, the challenging question is, how do we define a city from a sustainable services perspective, and to what does that definition refer?

Types of City Services

City or municipal services usually refer to the services that city authorities provide mainly to the city's residents. Yet cities typically offer numerous additional types of services that are produced, delivered, and used in the city by a variety of other providers and customers who are not necessarily citizens of the city. In general, all the services provided within the city framework can be divided—based on the nature of the service, the provider, the customer, and the platform, or the infrastructure upon which the service provision is based—into four main categories.

1. Municipal services—Public services provided by city authorities via different bodies and systems, and services that, although privatized, are still supervised and controlled by the city (Joassart-Marcelli and Musso 2005; Kelly and Swindell 2002). These include services that support the supply of physical resources or tangible values, such as water and electricity supplies and sewage removal, or intangible values such as governance, education, health, and welfare services.

2. Community services—Not-for-profit public services, from military service to soup kitchens, provided by individuals or by groups of people for benefit of the greater public (Youniss et al. 1999).

3. Private services—Provided by the private sector, individuals, or companies, private services span the entire spectrum of services, from food and clothing shops to medical services to equipment repair services.

4. Ecosystem services—Natural services ranging from temperature control and disease control to waste decomposition and human inspiration (Gretchen 1997).

The growing number and diversity of services provided by cities have elicited the need to integrate city services not only to optimize their provision and maximize their quality, but also to ensure their sustainability. In so doing, the local and global effects of services must be considered in the short and the long term. In the urban framework, sustainability refers to the integration of all the components and dimensions of the totality of urban activities and services to enable all stakeholders, including future generations, to enjoy high-quality life. Essential to this notion of sustainability is the continuity and prosperity of ecosystems over time, which can only be realized by limiting—or, ideally, preventing—damage to both the natural and the social environments that are integral to the city's existence (Davies et al. 2011; Zang, Wu, and Na 2011).

As mentioned previously, under the auspices of urban sustainability, local authorities around the globe are embracing new urban models—e.g., green city, ecocity, resilient city, or smart city—to cope with today's modern urban challenges. Both the green city and the ecocity concepts usually describe the rational use and regeneration of resources while reducing pollutant emissions and maintaining the health of both the social and the natural environments. Improving on that definition, the notion of a resilient city refers to the ability of a city to adapt to changes while providing the resources needed by its current inhabitants without infringing on its capacity to deliver the same resources to its future inhabitants. The resilient city thus maintains its "competitive edge," which facilitates the city's continued prosperity as a living space and as a place for business and leisure. Integrating these concepts into a comprehensive framework, the smart city combines information and communication technologies with sustainable urban development. But the management, planning, development, and operation of sustainable urban environments centered on the interplay between both the human and physical environments and the natural and built environments must reinvent how services are delivered and consumed within the city. Moreover, to address these challenges while considering sustainability as a service (Wolfson et al. 2010; Wolfson 2016), both the characteristics of a city and its physical boundaries must be redefined, and the different services of the city, as well as the role and responsibility of each stakeholder in their design and manufacture, must be identified and characterized. In short, to realize urban sustainability will require the redefinition of the city as a service-city.

The Service-City

Given the opportunity to create our cities from scratch, we would most likely build their physical structures and design their services using strategies markedly different from the less directed or conscious approaches used in the past. Yet because today few opportunities exist to build completely new cities, the trend in most of the world has been to modify current cities by enlarging them into megacities or metropolises. The service-city model, therefore, should be designed and developed from a perspective that considers the services and systems currently provided by the city while offering additional services that, together with existing services, are managed and operated using novel platforms.

Boundaries

The first step in designing the service-city model is to define its physical boundaries. A definition of the service-city's boundaries, however, must consider the essence of services; namely, services are produced and delivered at a time and place where both the provider and the customer meet (i.e., service's inseparability), and they are perishable and cannot be stored or reproduced in exactly the same way. From this point of view, the most straightforward definition of the service-city's physical boundaries is the area where the services are provided and used. For example, corresponding to this definition, municipal services were traditionally produced and delivered within the physical boundaries of the city for its residents, who were the service's main beneficiaries. The very nature of cities, however, dictates that some customers of a service are visitors from outside the city, and as such, they do not always use the service in the same place where it was provided. For instance, a patient who sees a doctor in a facility located in a certain city can act on the doctor's advice in another place. In addition, a significant part of today's marketplace is conducted in the virtual realm, where provider and customer typically do not meet in person, and they are not necessarily located in the same place. For example, a company's call center can be situated in one location from where it provides a service to customers who reside elsewhere. In this scenario—where the delivery of the service is actually performed in two different places—the main question becomes, to which place is the service ascribed: to where it was produced or to where it was used?

The answer to this question, it seems, depends on the effects that the service has on each place, including economic effects, such as on economic growth and the labor market; social effects, such as on the community; and environmental effects, such as the service's contribution to greenhouse gas emissions and air pollution and its influence on biodiversity.

Provision of the service, therefore, may enhance the economic activity of the provider's city, while the consumption of the service and its corresponding effects on the environment will be felt most strongly in the city where the customer resides. In this respect, every service delivery within the city's physical borders, including services that were transferred using virtual tools (even if they were produced and used in two different places), constitutes a part of the city's total services.

Provider and Customer

In general, everyone contributes in some way to the cocreation of city services. Therefore, the actors in the service system who play important roles include a variety of entities, which can be generally classified as providers, customers, city authorities, residents, visitors, and members of business from the private sector. More generally, the provider or the customer can also be a nonhuman entity, from nature to a computer and other instruments (owned and maintained by some responsible entity). In addition, for a variety of services, the customer may also simultaneously become a provider during the same service provision. Numerous smartphone applications, for example, fall into this category: Moovit, a public transportation application that aims to help customers optimally satisfy their transportation needs, uses the information entered by each customer to update in real time the information it supplies to all of its customers, making that customer a provider of information to the service's other customers. The potential variety and diversity of both providers and customers within the city poses a major logistical challenge. That challenge manifests in the organization and integration of all the relevant players and in the creation and support of a reliable and dependable platform that encourages the production and provision of both general and specific services. Furthermore, that platform should be accessible to, and fulfill the requirements of, every provider and customer.

Value

The value of a service can be initiated by the provider, the customer, or both. As such, the service can be oriented either in a top-down fashion, from the city to the resident and other stakeholders, or in a bottom-up scenario, from the residents or the private sector to the city or between a resident and a member of the private sector or between the residents themselves.

The service-city should comprise three different value provision models: (i) value in-exchange, which is value transferred from a supplier to a consumer; (ii) value in-use, which is value cocreated between a provider and a customer; and (iii) value in-return, which is value cogenerated by a provider and customer for other stakeholders. In addition, to sustainably provide all values (i.e., sustainable service), the economic, social, and environmental dimensions and effects of each service provision should be considered. In this respect, social values are those that account for justice, equity, and the stability of social order. Moreover, they should match the "needs" and "haves" not only of individuals, but also of communities. Economic value should consider the variety of economic models, such as cooperative and share economies, which, when incorporated into the local economy, function to strengthen it. Lastly, environmental value should extend beyond physical resource management and the use of cleantechs (Pernick and Wilder 2007) and CleanServs (Wolfson, Tavor, and Mark 2013a, 2014; Wolfson et al. 2015) to include a life cycle perspective and resiliency (i.e., sustainability cycle). Finally, the values that are provided in the frame of the service-city must permeate the entire value hierarchy—i.e., DIKIW: (Ackoff 1989; Spohrer, Piciocchi, and Bassano 2012)—from the collection of data to the processing of information into knowledge to the production of intelligent solutions that increase process efficiency and that eventually generate wisdom to increase effectiveness.

Whole or Holistic Service

Recently, the related concepts of whole and holistic service systems were introduced in the framework of service science in terms of service-dominant logic (Demirkan, Spohrer, and Krishna 2011; Spohrer 2011). A whole service can be defined as a service system or a service network that provides its customers with all the services they need—for example, a city, a luxury hotel, and so on. A closed service atmosphere, the whole service system facilitates, on the one hand, the rebuilding or the initial construction of a variety of entities, from cities to societies. On the other hand, it can also be used to preserve established values that may still have merit (Wolfson 2016). Insofar as it is equally applicable to the integration of environmental, social, and economic values within either existing or new networks, the whole service system is also the ideal framework within which to introduce sustainability as service.

Similar to the whole service model, the holistic service system can also support the entirety of people's needs and provide them with all the tangible and intangible values they require or want. However, the boundaries of the holistic service system extend beyond those of the whole service system, as the former deals with both the efficiency with which the various services within the whole service system are provided and the level of completeness, independence, and extended duration of the whole service system. Completeness refers to the quality of life the system delivers in terms of supplying the resources people need while developing and maintaining infrastructure and while creating and implementing economic, health, and education systems and systems of governance. The level of independence of a whole service is assessed based on the extent to which it does not require the support of external service systems. The level of extended duration of a whole service can be defined for a whole service that is supplied for only a short period of time or one that is provided indefinitely (e.g., whole services such as smart cities). In the framework of the holistic service system, therefore, the various services supplied by a provider must also be interconnected. Moreover, customers must cocreate the value while perpetuating the service atmosphere in a manner analogous to how ecosystem services function, thereby yielding sustainability as in the model of the sustainable city. A sustainable service network, therefore, is that which holistically considers the entire service system and not only its individual services. Likewise, a sustainable service network necessarily involves the sharing of physical and nonphysical resources, the renewal of those resources in cyclical processes, and the rebuilding of societal infrastructure.

The main characteristics of a city as a whole service or as a holistic service and the difference between the two are summarized in Table 5.1.

Table 5.1 City characteristics in terms of whole service and holistic service

	Whole	Holistic
Physical boundaries	Place	Environment
Human boundaries	People/individuals	Community
Provider	Mainly the city	Everyone
Customer	Mainly the residents	Everyone
Value hierarchy	Mainly information and knowledge	From information to wisdom
Value dimensions	Economic, social, and environmental values	Sustainable values
Value models	Value in-exchange and value in-use	Value in-exchange, value in-use, and value in-return
Integration	Unconnected services	Connected services

Service-City Architecture

To implement the service-city model, the design, provision, and use of each service in the city should be built and synchronized using a unique architecture (Figures 5.1 and 5.2). This architecture comprises the three horizontal layers of design (Figure 5.1a), provisioning (Figure 5.1b), and sustainability (Figure 5.1c) and the two cross-cutting, vertical layers of integration and control (Figure 5.2).

The horizontal layers of the service-city architecture are applied sequentially when implementing the service-city model. Beginning with the design layer, both provider and customer are chosen from among the four options of city, residents, private sector, or other, and the level of hierarchy is chosen from the DIKIW pyramid (Ackoff 1989; Spohrer, Piciocchi, and Bassano 2012). Progressing to the second layer, provision is decided by choosing the appropriate value provision model (e.g., in-exchange, in-use, or in-return) and mode of operation (e.g., self, super, or mixed). In the last horizontal layer of sustainability, the social, environmental, and economic dimensions that are essential to the value should be defined while considering all short- and long-term and local and global effects and the influence that these will have on both individuals and societies. Finally, the three horizontal layers are integrated and controlled

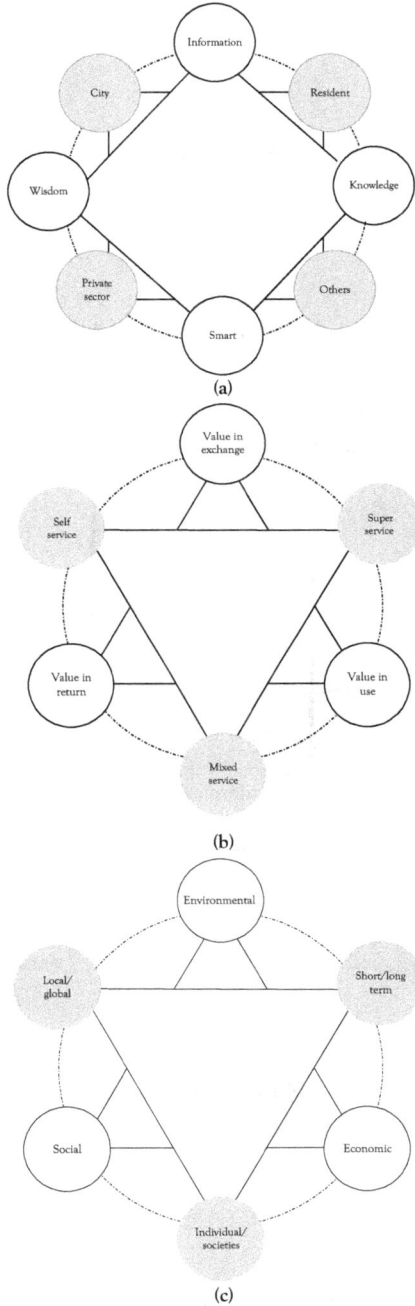

Figure 5.1 Horizontal layers of service-city architecture: (a) design, (b) sustainability, and (c) provision

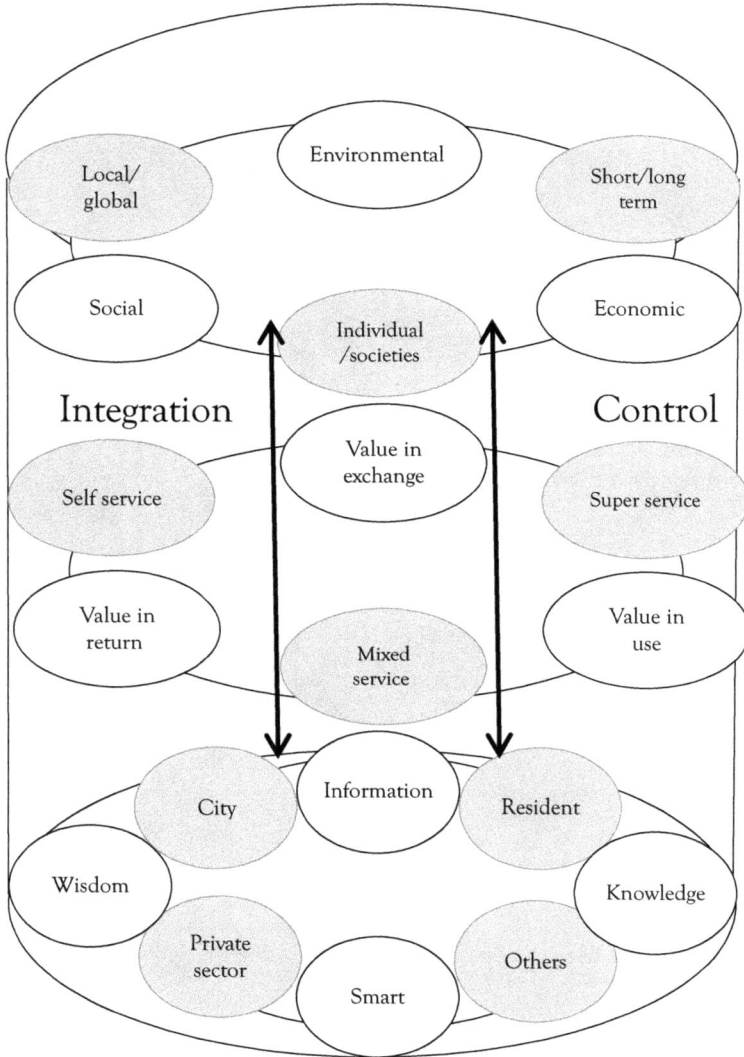

Figure 5.2 Vertical layers of integration and control in the service-city architecture

by the addition of supporting services such as regulations, and so on. (Figure 5.2).

The service-city model should also be imbued with circularity as an integral part of its design. Indeed, the notion of circularity should be built into each horizontal and vertical layer (i.e., in the design and provision of each individual service as well as in the integration of some services). Additionally, it should be incorporated as an essential part of the framework for holistic service systems, thereby transforming the service-city model from a two-dimensional to a three-dimensional model. As such, each service will be produced and provided while considering multiplicities of providers and customers, direct and indirect, to ensure the circularity of all the service's tangible and intangible values. This approach, in turn, facilitates the efficiency and effectiveness of each service provision as well as of the entire system. In the following chapter, some examples of the service-city are presented.

CHAPTER 6

Service-City Examples

The service-city model was conceptualized to improve municipal services and their management by integrating the numerous services offered by the city under one umbrella. It is designed to interconnect human behavior, well-being, and other social dimensions with important environmental aspects, such as resource utilization and the emission of pollution, via infrastructures and technologies. Though this complex structure would be easiest to build from scratch, the opportunities to do so, such as the establishment of completely new cities, are rare. The service-city model is instead applied to the restructuring of the service architectures of existing cities, a challenge of infinitely greater proportions insofar as it necessitates imbuing conventional municipal activities with both service and sustainability features.

Electronic Governance

Principal among the challenges facing the city of today is the allocation, control, and management of its physical and nonphysical resources. This process requires a set of policies, procedures, mechanisms, and units, which can be defined as governance and assembled under the umbrella of administrative authority. The changing nature of cities requires also the redesigning of municipal governance, and linking people, communities, organizations, companies, and regulatory practices to streamline the assignment and distribution of goods and services. In this respect, and with the new opportunities enabled by the advent of ICTs, many cities have adopted the use of electronic services, which comprise technology-based communication, coordination, and interaction processes in municipal governance (i.e., electronic governance or e-governance). The concept of e-governance often overlaps that of e-government, which refers to the use of ICTs in public administration to improve public services. Yet, although the two terms are often treated as essentially the same, some have distinguished between the two. For example, Rossel and Finger (2007) argued that while e-government only uses ICT to help governing, e-governance refers to technologies that both promote governance and that have to be governed. Palvia and Sharma (2007), on the other hand, claimed that the focus of e-government is on constituencies and stakeholders outside the organization, including the government or public sector at the city, county, state, national, or international level, while e-governance focuses on administration and management within an organization, public or private, large or small.

In addition to the desire to exploit advanced technologies to promote smoother city governance, the main drivers behind the move from governance to e-governance are to (1) combat bureaucratic governance, (2) offer more citizen-centric governance, (3) streamline and increase the effectivity of governance, (4) reduce operational cost and response time, and (5) add innovation and entrepreneurship. UNESCO defines e-governance from a broader perspective as the public sector's use of ICTs with the aim of improving information and service delivery, encouraging citizen participation in the decision-making process, and making government more accountable, transparent, and effective. E-governance involves new styles of leadership, new ways of debating and deciding policy and investment, new ways of accessing education, new ways of listening to citizens, and new ways of organizing and delivering information and services. E-governance is generally considered a wider concept than e-government, since it can bring about a change in the way citizens relate to governments and to each other. E-governance can bring forth new concepts of citizenship, in terms of both citizen needs and citizen responsibilities. Its objective is to engage, enable, and empower the citizen (Information Resources Management Association 2014).

Types of E-Government

E-government services are usually grouped into four categories according to the type of interaction (Alshehri and Drew 2010):

1. Government to citizen (G2C)—An external interface that covers the majority of interactions between the government and citizens.

It enables the government to make its large range of public services available and accessible and it allows the citizen to choose when and where to interact with the government, thus improving the quality of these services.

2. Government to business (G2B)—An external platform that includes various services exchanged between government and the business sector. It cuts costs, saves time, and creates a more transparent business environment to increase business performance efficiency.

3. Government to government (G2G)—An internal system that promotes increased flow of information and services within and between the different government entities.

4. Government to employee (G2E)—An internal scheme that facilitates greater interaction between government authorities and their employees.

Government services in the e-governance model function according to a four-stage process comprising information, interaction, transaction, and transformation. In addition, each increase in stage also increases the level of the value in the value pyramid and the complexity of the technology being employed by the service.

1. The first stage of information involves the creation by authorities of a website that enables them to provide citizens (G2C) and businesses (G2B) with relevant information, from the types of services offered by city authorities and the benefits, requirements, and schedules of each to the advertisement of municipal-sponsored performances and events. This stage also includes the provision of internal information for other municipal entities (G2G) and for employees (G2E). In terms of service models, this stage can be attributed mainly to value in-exchange.

2. The second stage of interaction allows citizens (G2C), businesses (G2B), and municipal agents or entities (G2G) to interact with the authority over a dedicated website that enables one to post questions and to download municipal forms and documents. In terms of service models, this stage can be attributed mainly to the value in-use model.

3. The third stage of transaction involves the exchange of more than information and allows more complex interactions with the customer (G2C and G2B). Payment of taxes and the issuing of documents such as applications for building licenses or to install new signage are included in the frame of this stage. This stage can also be attributed mainly to the value in-use model.

4. The fourth stage of transformation enables the production and provision of integrated services (G2C and G2B) in which, although more than one department or municipal entity is involved, the service is provided as a "one-stop" solution by a single municipal body. This stage, which requires greater interaction and coordination between the municipal departments, includes services such as the issuing of birth certificates, which requires interaction between the health and civil services departments. This stage can be provided via both the value in-exchange and the value in-use models.

The e-governance platform allows efficient, effective, and customer-oriented electronic and interactive services that can be easily accessed from anywhere 24 hours a day, 7 days a week. It usually requires fewer physical and nonphysical resources (e.g., gasoline, time, etc.), and it is typically more accessible and cost-effective, thereby providing a more sustainable solution. Despite their many apparent benefits, however, e-services are not necessarily suitable to or accessible by everyone. Therefore, although the demand for conventional service options based on human interaction will be greatly reduced, they should nevertheless be continued, albeit on a less intense scale.

An additional benefit of using an e-governance platform is that it is not limited to unidirectional interaction that proceeds from the municipal authorities to the public (Ntiro 2000). Additionally, it can also be used as a platform that allows the public to initiate or even to supply services, thereby expanding the interactive possibilities to include citizens or businesses to government (C2G or B2G) or any other stakeholders and even between them (C2B, B2C, B2B, C2C) (Figure 6.1). This type of interaction promotes improved city governance and facilitates circularity, as it allows the customer to become a provider via a value in-return model. It includes, for example, not only feedback from the citizens or

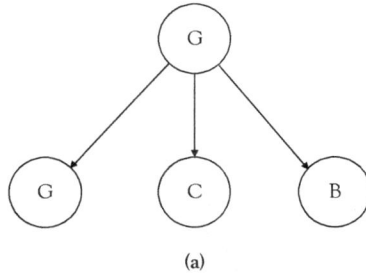

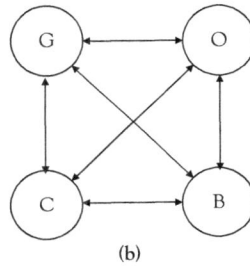

G-government, C-citizen, B-businesses, O-others

Figure 6.1 E-governance models: (a) traditional model, (b) offered model

businesses to the municipality regarding the city's e-governance services, but also services that citizens or businesses provide to the city or to each other to facilitate governance. For example, businesses can function as a third party that provides government services, such as the issuance of car licenses, to citizens. Finally, the e-governance model can also allow new interactions between city e-governance entities and various city stakeholders other than citizens or local businesses, such as tourists or noncitizen students. For example, the city website can be used by anyone to obtain information about local events and by national or even international accreditation agencies to provide local businesses with certification regarding their ecological or social performance.

Sustainable Urban Transport Service

Transportation, one of the most widespread activities in our daily lives and a defining characteristic of modern life, especially in the city, is necessary for both economic and social development. Yet the production, use, and maintenance of the wide variety of vehicular means of transportation built today and their eventual disposal at the end of their economic life are associated with heavy environmental pollution and the consumption of vast quantities of natural resources. In addition, the building and maintenance of the infrastructure required for transportation are also associated with a decidedly negative environmental impact (Wolfson 2016).

Our widespread reliance on gasoline-based private cars, perhaps the most popular means of transportation in developed countries, is responsible for a significant proportion of the environmental damage associated with the transport sector. The numbers of motor vehicles per capita in OECD countries averages 30 vehicles per 100 inhabitants (OECD 2009), and it varies worldwide from 25 vehicles per 100 inhabitants in Turkey to 80 vehicles per 100 inhabitants in the United States (NationMaster 2014). Indeed, the environmental damage wrought by our excessive use of private vehicles (e.g., cars, motorcycles, etc.) dictates that more sustainable transportation solutions be developed and offered.

In general, the goal of sustainable transport can be realized via three types of service: (1) replacement of the gasoline-powered private car with more sustainable means of transport, including private alternatives such as bicycles and electric cars and public endeavors such as bus and train systems; (2) addition of supporting services for private cars (i.e., product-service systems or PSSs), for instance, car rental and carpooling; and (3) addition of supporting services that regulate or control the traffic, such as traffic laws, toll roads, traffic lights, and so on. But to achieve the goal of sustainable transport, all transportation means and services should be synchronized and matched with other city activities and services relevant to the transport sector. These include obvious activities, such as road maintenance and municipal garbage collection services, but they should also include other factors, such as information about weather conditions, traffic congestion, and motor vehicle accidents.

According to the service-city model, the various services within the city should be listed and characterized on the basis of the model dimensions (Chapter 5, Figures 5.1 and 5.2). Services in the transport market can be categorized according to five different types, organized into two main groups on the basis of the essence of the solution each offers:

A. Transportation solutions (horizontal layers in the model):

1. Private transportation, including cars and motorcycles, but also walking and bicycles. Although these solutions are not services by definition, their use supplies a type of service (i.e., movement from one location to another).
2. Public transportation via different PSSs, from bus and train to carpooling and carsharing.

B. Supportive services (vertical layers in the model):

1. Traffic regulation applications that facilitate the efficient operation of the various solutions and their combinations—for example, real-time images of current traffic conditions and information about public transportation availability.
2. Regulation and control services, from traffic lights and high-occupancy vehicle lanes for public transportation to traffic laws.
3. Supporting services that promote better traffic flow, such as infrastructure maintenance and rapid accident response systems.

Table 6.1 lists the different transport solutions and summarizes the dimensions of each with respect to the first two layers of the service-city model [i.e., design and provision (Chapter 5, Figures 5.1a and 5.1b)].

Table 6.1 Dimensions of the various transportation solutions based on design and provision layers

Solution/ Service	Provider	Customer	DIKIW	Service Model	Service Mode
Private transportation					
Motor vehicle: car, motorcycle, etc.	Residents	Residents	-	-	-
Bicycle	Residents	Residents	-	-	-
Walking	Residents	Residents	-	-	-

(Continued)

Table 6.1 (Continued)

Solution/ Service	Provider	Customer	DIKIW	Service Model	Service Mode
Public transportation					
Bus	Private sector/City	Residents	Intelligence	In use-Cousage	Super
Train	Private sector/City	Residents	Intelligence	In use-Cousage	Super
Tram	Private sector/City	Residents	Intelligence	In use-Cousage	Super
Taxi	Private sector	Residents	Intelligence	In use-Coproduce	Mixed
Carpool application (Uber)	Residents	Residents	Wisdom	In use-Coproduce	Self
Carsharing	Residents	Residents	Wisdom	In use-Codesign	Self
Carpool	Residents	Residents	Wisdom	In use-Codesign	Self
Rental car	Private sector	Residents	Intelligence	In use-Coproduce	Mixed
Rental bicycle	Private sector/City	Residents	Intelligence	In use-Coproduce	Mixed
Traffic regulation applications					
Real-time picture of traffic (Waze or Google Maps)	Private sector/ Residents	Residents/ Private sector	Wisdom	In use-Codesign (In return)	Self
Real-time picture of public transportation (Moovit)	Private sector/ Residents	Residents/ Private sector	Wisdom	In use-Codesign (In return)	Self
Regulation and control services					
Traffic lights	City	Residents/ Private sector	Intelligence	In exchange	Super
Smart card	Private sector/City	Residents/ Private sector	Intelligence	In use-Coproduce	Self

Solution/ Service	Provider	Customer	DIKIW	Service Model	Service Mode
Regulation: Toll road	Private sector/City	Residents/ Private sector	Knowledge	In exchange	Super
Public transportation free-line	Private sector/City	Residents/ Private sector	Knowledge	In exchange	Super
Regulation: Laws	City	Residents/ Private sector	Knowledge	In exchange	Super
Other supporting services					
Infrastructures	City	Residents/ Private sector	Intelligence	In exchange	Super
Parking	Private sector/City	Residents/ Private sector	Intelligence	In use- Co-use	Mixed
Weather forecast	Private sector	Residents/ Private sector	Information	In exchange	Super
Accidents information	Private sector/City	Residents	Information	In exchange	Super

According to the service-city model, the sustainability of each service from the environmental, social, and economic perspectives should also be characterized. To do so, the first step is to identify the main goals of the transportation market. Table 6.2 summarizes the primary goals of sustainable transport based on a survey of the literature.

Table 6.2 Main goals of sustainable transport (Litman 2007)

Aspect	Goals
Economic	Increased economic development Increased efficiency and productivity Development of the local economy
Environmental	Reduced air, water, land, and noise pollution Decreased greenhouse gas emissions Increased resource conservation Protection of biodiversity and open spaces
Social	Increased equity, affordability, human safety and health, and local community cohesion

The primary goals of sustainable transport then need to be analyzed and formulated in terms of the concrete actions that must be taken to realize each goal. These actions, or potential solutions, are then compared, on the basis of which sustainability indicators, or understandable and manageable numbers that capture the key issues and their complex inter-relationships, should be selected.

Over the relatively short history of sustainability science, a range of different indicators have been introduced to measure the sustainability of products or processes. Besides the difficulties entailed in obtaining reli-able and comparative numbers, practitioners have been hard pressed to identify a single, comparative number that encompasses all the aspects of sustainability, as each indicator is calculated using different scales, dimen-sions, and weight. Moreover, though there are already various measures for quantifying the sustainability of a process or a product, most of them are based exclusively on the environmental aspects of sustainability (i.e., resource consumption, pollution emission, and waste generation), as expressed, for example, by the ecological footprint (Wackernagel and Rees 1998) or environmental sustainability index (Schmiedeknecht 2013). Insofar as sustainability comprises economic and social dimensions in addition to its environmental component, sustainability measures must account for the impacts of all three of these components.

As stated previously, the goal of a sustainability assessment of a service is to identify the available options for performing the service and then to compare them in terms of the sustainability of each to determine the most sustainable option. However, as the quantity of each indicator can vary across a huge range between the services, the relative weight of each indica-tor should also be considered (Wolfson 2016). Based on surveys of the lit-erature and some leading experts in the field, four indicators were created (Table 6.3) for assessments of sustainability based on its environmental, social, and economic dimensions. Services can be assessed for their overall sustainability on the basis of these indicators, which for a given service are rated from 0 (best impact) to 5 (worst impact) on a Likert-type scale that reflects the service's impact on each dimension of sustainability relative to that of comparable alternatives. In addition, while for certain indica-tors, such as greenhouse gas emissions, the lower the number the greater the effect; for other indicators, such as safety, the higher the number the greater the effect. In the frame of this study, therefore, both the solution with the highest greenhouse gas emissions and that with the lowest safety ranking received a value of 5. In addition, as the value of each indicator is also dependent on where (the place) and when (the time) the service was performed, numbers from representative examples in the literature were used in the frame of this assessment. Finally, as the corresponding weight of each indicator is also difficult to determine, in the frame of this example the sustainability impact of the whole solution, for either private or public transportation, was calculated by simple average, whereby each indicator was assigned the same weight. Lastly, the addition of regulating or supporting services to the different means of transportation is expected to change their overall rankings on the basis of interactions between the relevant supporting and main services. For example, using the Moovit application improves the social and environmental impacts of using public transport, as it allows customers to match their transportation needs with the most suitable transport solution and to send real-time updates about the service (e.g., whether it's running on time). Using Moovit can therefore also enhance the experience of other users of public transport and increase people's reliance on it, thereby reducing per capita emission levels, but it does not affect the users of private vehicles.

Sustainability indicators were calculated on the basis of following assumptions:

1. The comparison was done per passenger per km during rush hour.
2. Private transportation and any corresponding PSS (e.g., taxi, car rental/leasing) were based on the journey of a single passenger, while public transportation and carpooling were considered for full passenger capacities.
3. A PSS involving a car, such as carsharing, was assumed to be used at full capacity, 24 hours a day/7 days a week, while private cars were assumed to be in use 5 to 10 percent of the time (Kenworthy and Laube 2001; Vivier 2006).

A. **Environmental sustainability indicators** (Table 6.3):

1. **Air pollution** (the lower the better)—Ranking is based on operational and nonoperational environmental assessments of passenger transportation in the different transportation modes for which

SOx, NO$_X$, CO, and Volatile Organic Compounds (VOC) emissions are measured (Chester and Arpad 2009).

2. **Greenhouse gas emissions** (the lower the better)—Ranking is based on operational and nonoperational environmental assessments of passenger transportation in the various transportation modes (Chester and Arpad 2009).

3. **Resource efficiency** (the higher the better)—Calculation is based on energy used in operational and nonoperational environmental assessments of passenger transportation in various transportation modes (Chester and Arpad 2009) and the level of usage of each means of transportation (Vivier 2006).

4. **Noise pollution** (the lower the better)—Measures a similar effect of each of the motor-based means of transportation. The greater the number of passengers per means of transportation, the lower the value.

Table 6.3 Environmental sustainability indicators

Solution/ Service	Air pollution	Green- house gas emissions	Resource efficiency	Noise pollution	Sum
Private transportation					
Motor vehicle: car, motorcycle, etc.	5	5	5	5	5
Bicycle	0	0	1	0	0.25
Walking	0	0	1	0	0.25
Public transportation					
Bus	3	3	2	2	2.5
Train	2	2	2	1	1.75
Tram	2	2	2	1	1.75
Taxi	4	4	3	4	3.75
Carpool application (Uber)	4	4	2	4	3.5
Carsharing	4	4	3	4	3.75
Carpool	3	3	3	4	3.25
Rental car	4	4	4	5	4.25
Rental bike	0	0	1	0	0.25

Another important environmental indicator is **habitat protection** (the higher the better), but as it is very difficult to measure, its calculation is usually based on land-use measures that are considered among the economic indicators used in the same assessment.

B. **Social sustainability indicators** (Table 6.4):

1. **Safety** (the higher the better)—Based on passenger fatality rates (American Public Transportation Association 2015).
2. **Affordability** (the higher the better)—Based on car ownership, the availability of each service, and its price per use.
3. **Accessibility** (the higher the better)—Based on infrastructure (access pathways to and location of public transport stations, etc).
4. **Equity** (the higher the better)—Based on car ownership, the availability of each service, its price per use, and the quality of service-related infrastructures.

Table 6.4 Social sustainability indicators

Solution/ Service	Safety	Affordability	Accessibility	Equity	Sum
Private transportation					
Motor vehicle: car, motorcycle, etc.	5	1	5	1	3
Bicycle	3	5	4	5	4.25
Walking	3	5	4	5	4.25
Public transportation					
Bus	1	5	4	5	3.75
Train	1	5	3	5	3.5
Tram	1	5	3	5	3.5
Taxi	5	4	4	3	4
Carpool application (Uber)	5	4	4	3	4
Carsharing	5	2	2	2	2.75
Carpool	5	2	2	2	2.75
Rental car	5	2	2	2	2.74
Rental bike	3	4	4	4	3.75

Another important social indicator for sustainability assessments is **user satisfaction** (the higher the better), but similar to habitat protection, it does not lend itself to easy measurement, because the numbers needed to reliably compare the different services for comparable scenarios are difficult to identify.

C. **Economic sustainability indicators** (Table 6.5):

1. **Commute time** (the lower the better)—Daily average travel time (Hitge and Vanderschuren 2015).
2. **Cost per passenger-km** (the lower the better)—Internal and external costs, from infrastructure and operational costs to air and noise pollution costs to the costs associated with accidents (Glazebrook 2009).
3. **Expenses per revenue** (the lower the better)—Capital (facilities, equipment, and other durable goods) and operational (labor, fuel, and maintenance) expenses divided by revenues (Litman 2015).

Table 6.5 Economic sustainability indicators

Solution/ Service	Commute time	Cost to passenger	Expenses per revenue	Land use	Sum
Private transportation					
Motor vehicle: car, motorcycle, etc.	4	5	5	5	4.75
Bicycle	5	0	0	2	1.75
Walking	5	0	0	1	1.5
Public transportation					
Bus	3	2	3	4	3
Train	2	2	2	2	2
Tram	2	2	2	2	2
Taxi	4	5	4	5	4.5
Carpool application (Uber)	4	4	4	5	4.25
Carsharing	4	4	4	5	4.25
Carpool	4	3	3	4	3.5
Rental car	4	5	4	5	4.5
Rental bike	5	1	1	2	2.25

4. **Land use** (the lower the better)—The different ways that human beings use and manage the land and its resources (Statistics Sweden 2010).

The overall sustainability of each solution was calculated by simple average, in which each indicator was assigned the same weight (Table 6.6). Because the Likert scale reflects the indicator's impact on a given dimension of sustainability ranges from 0 (best impact) to 5 (worst impact), the lower the overall score, the greater the sustainability.

The sustainability of each solution can be further influenced by the addition of supportive services (vertical layers in the model) (Chapter 5, Figure 5.1b), such as public transport apps or traffic regulations. Indeed, the combination of a means of transportation with a supporting service can reduce its overall sustainability score by as much as 1 to 3 points. For instance, the addition to roadways of a lane reserved for public transport can tremendously reduce the time of the journey and the corresponding air pollution and greenhouse gas emissions while increasing its resource efficiency, thereby

Table 6.6 Overall sustainability score

Solution/Service	Sustainability
Private transportation	
Motor vehicle: car, motorcycle, etc.	4.25
Bicycle	2.08
Walking	2
Public transportation	
Bus	3.08
Train	2.42
Tram	2.42
Taxi	4.08
Carpool application (Uber)	3.92
Carsharing (ZipCar)	3.58
Carpool	3.17
Rental car	3.83
Rental bike	2.08

reducing the overall sustainability score of a solution such as a public bus from 3.08 to 2.08. Similarly, using Waze allows one to reduce the time, air pollution, and greenhouse gas emissions associated with solutions such as the bus, the car, and carpooling.

However, to achieve the goal of sustainable circular services within the city, the services used in the transportation sector should be coordinated with those in other sectors. For instance, the heavy traffic during the morning rush hour increases pollution levels and the cost per journey due to the increased time vehicles spend on the road and their corresponding use of more gasoline per kilometer. However, to ameliorate the detrimental effects of morning rush-hour traffic on sustainability, the performance of certain services that are provided in the city could be scheduled outside the rush hour. For example, the start of the school day, the distribution of merchandise to stores, and waste collection could all be scheduled outside the hours of 7:00 to 10:00 in the morning.

CHAPTER 7

Virtual Environment

One of the main drivers of the changes that humans have made to the natural environment and that is behind the creation of the human environment is the construction of cities. As they look toward the future, however, the cities of today also have to consider the development of the *virtual environment* (Kalawsky 1993; Rix, Haas, and Teixeira 2016). In the last decade, the field of virtual technologies (i.e., those that are used to develop imaginary or virtual worlds alongside the real physical world) has grown exponentially. In contrast to the physical world—where physical matter is seen, touched, and ingested—the virtual world is a symbolic one in which computer programs provide functionality and massive amounts of data can be transferred. Moreover, in the virtual world, time and space and social and economic concepts gain new meanings, and they are not subject to the physical laws or to the ethical rules that exist in the real world.

Virtual-World Technologies

The two main technologies being used today in the framework of the virtual world are virtual reality (VR) and augmented reality (AR). VR refers to an artificial, computer-generated simulation or recreation of a real-life environment or situation (Biocca and Levy 2013; Earnshaw 2014; Loomis 2016). These so-called virtual environments are experienced by users through their personal devices, such as computers, mobile phones, and dedicated glasses, which allow users to undergo experiences that they cannot have in the real world. Currently, VR is used mainly to enhance imaginary realities for gaming and entertainment and to create simulations of reality (e.g., for training exercises undertaken to prepare for real-life environments). In contrast, augmented-reality technologies apply computer-generated layers on top of an existing reality to render a more meaningful experience for the user during interaction (Lin et al. 2017; Billinghurst, Clark, and Lee 2015). Insofar as it merges the real world with virtual worlds, this type of technology is also referred to as mixed, dual, or hybrid reality (Ohta and Tamura 2014). Based on the combination of virtual sounds and images with real-world elements, it is widely used, for example, as a study aid, to enhance gaming, and to provide empowering experiences. Although VR constructs a new world while AR uses the existing world, the two technologies have much in common. Both rely on the same technologies, which enable them to reach people anywhere, and both were developed with the shared objective of enhancing people's experiences.

From the perspective of sustainability, virtual-world technologies must be considered in terms of their social, environmental, and economic effects, all of which are still under investigation. Arguably, both VR and AR technologies are having short- and long-term effects on individuals and societies at the local and global levels (Figure 2.1). Participation in the virtual world has many social benefits, among them the ability to initiate new social interactions, the increase in communication options, the promotion of feeling of inclusion from being part of a group, and the opportunity to use one's skills to actively contribute to social services such as education (Thorsteinsson 2013; Ott and Freina 2015), well-being (Crespo et al. 2016), medicine (Pedersen 2014), and psychotherapy (Anderson et al. 2013). But the virtual environment has also changed how people interact and communicate (Kiesler 2014). In fact, in some scenarios, the virtual world may also be a cause for major concern, as the technologies it exploits have the potential to disrupt social order (e.g., justice and laws) and to isolate people from each other. As people become increasingly invested in their virtual environments, their initially naive use of the technology can develop into an addiction to an unhealthy escape from reality. Likewise, the creators of these virtual environments can exploit their technology to control the minds and experiences of their users (Hartanto et al. 2014; Weisel 2015).

Though virtual-world technologies themselves require relatively small quantities of natural resources, they have potentially deleterious environmental effects (Brown and Green 2016). The short shelf life of computers, mobile phones, and similar devices and the construction of these devices using nonrenewable metals and oxides should arouse great concern. In addition, electromagnetic radiation from the various devices also poses health threat. Furthermore, the use of these devices in general and specifically as platforms for virtual or AR is driven mainly by people's wants (e.g., entertainment, leisure) and not by their basic needs (e.g., food and shelter). Lastly, the virtual environment may widen the already large gap between the natural and human environments.

Virtual World and Cities

The concepts and technologies behind virtual environments present the city with novel challenges (Nguyen et al. 2016). First and foremost, insofar as it generates a new and imaginary world that exists within the real world and that has far-reaching effects at both the individual and community levels, these technologies are expected to change the fundamental defining characteristics of future cities. Conceivably, people's experience and behavior in the physical world of future cities will probably be influenced by the virtual world and will depend to some extent on its intersection with the physical world. Furthermore, the desire of each person to use these technologies to build a virtual utopian city while tailoring infrastructures and services to their own needs will pose another challenge for most cities in the future.

Although the virtual world is necessarily reliant on the physical world for the materials and energy required to run computing systems, because it provides mainly intangible values, such as experience and learning, it is essentially a service. But virtual services are not limited to e-services that run on ICTs in the physical world as they create new worlds and generate new services. VR and AR technologies are also highly applicable to the production and provision of city services. For example, both technologies can be employed in city design and planning. In this respect, AR technologies can be exploited to visualize what a future structure will look like when it is built or to simulate traffic and even anticipate noise pollution levels, while VR technologies can be used in simulations to visualize how people will behave and interact in an as-yet-unbuilt area of the city—for example, a proposed community center or shopping center.

The services provided by ICTs and virtual-world technologies can also promote more efficient and effective decision-making processes and a better understanding of the relationship between people and location.

One of the most powerful yet simple tools for facilitating the interaction between information and location is the geographic information system (GIS), which has many applications across a range of city activities. In general, GIS technology organizes data on a map and allows users to select the data layers that are relevant to the task or project at hand and to display them on the map. For instance, a map that shows the age distribution of a city's residents can indicate to planners which city zones require more kindergartens and which need more centers dedicated to the city's elderly. The combination of GIS with virtual-reality technologies also enables city authorities to display pertinent city data on 3D maps—for example, the visualization of urban landscapes (e.g., buildings and streets) within GIS (Zhang and Moore 2014; Portman, Natapov, and Fisher-Gewirtzman 2015)—which can improve urban planning efforts and promote better decision making and the design of better cities. Virtual-reality GIS can also illustrate traffic data to present a real-time picture and enable more efficient driver navigation (Li et al. 2015). In addition, AR can also be embedded in a city's tourism marketing application that integrates virtual images with GIS and that provides tourists with location-specific information about suggested attractions and about relevant businesses,(e.g., restaurants, car rental agencies) (Lin et al. 2014).

Augmented or Virtual Reality and City Planning

Biljecki et al. (2015) reviewed the applications of 3D city models that use augmented- or virtual-reality technologies. They found that 3D city models are currently being used in dozens of application domains for diverse purposes, such as landscape and urban planning, shade effects and energy flow, mitigation plans that use mapping and visualization tools, and estimation of urban flood risks. Yet VR can also be used to learn about the behavior of residents or other stakeholders in the city. This technology can make public participation more accessible to the city's residents and improve the reliability of its results, thus having a direct impact on the planning process and its outcomes (Stauskis 2014; Simpson 2001).

Insofar as urban planning and subsequent decision making should encompass and interact with all the relevant social, economic, physical, and spatial considerations of any planning project, it is a very complex process. Indeed, it typically involves a range of stakeholders with different and often conflicting needs, expectations, and foci (e.g., local authority planners, planners of the clients, the clients themselves, and the general public), and all these competing views must be considered together (Hall 1996). The urban planning process is further complicated by the need for unique skills and abilities at the different stages of design and evaluation.

In general, an urban planning process is initiated through interaction between the city and the client, via the city planners or architects, to yield an agreed-upon plan. The plan is later presented to the general public via different routes (e.g., letters to residents, companies, and owners of neighboring properties and publication in the newspaper or on Internet sites), after which the general public, including individuals or organized groups of community representatives (e.g., local businesses or environmental groups), are invited to submit their objections to the plan. Although this mechanism of public participation is still limited, the transparency and sense of community inclusion afforded by considering the needs of all stakeholders when undertaking urban planning projects will help recruit community members as equal partners in the venture. Thus, in addition to the exchange of data and information, urban planning efforts that are implemented based on open communication between all the stakeholders should also create knowledge, intelligence, and, finally, wisdom to obtain smart value (Ackoff 1989).

To generate wisdom in urban planning efforts and obtain better end results, technological solutions such as VR can be exploited to improve urban planning processes and to enhance communication between the various stakeholders during the whole process. Supporting traditional 2D land-use maps and images (e.g., buildings and streets) with 3D models and multimedia, for instance, can be further enhanced by using augmented- and virtual-reality technologies that can more accurately reflect the complexity of an urban plan, from viewing its anticipated future built appearance to navigating in a virtual urban simulation. For example, the city of Perth in Australia built a 3D City Model over an area of 12 square kilometers. For use by the city departments involved in strategy, planning, and city design, the model boasts a level of detail that is accurate to 0.25 meters for terrain and to 0.5 meters for buildings.

VR can also be used to gain a sense of how people will behave and interact in the future project once it is built. For instance, the Department of Urban Design at Vilnius Gediminas Technical University in Lithuania, in partnership with the Vilnius City Municipality's Urban Development Department, used virtual urban simulation to study the extent to which the city's Missionaries Park project will match the interests of locals and of the entire city's community (Stauskis 2014). The goal of the project was to assess the extent to which the park's plan engaged with public attractiveness, functionality, safety, and security, and it was undertaken with the interests of a variety of stakeholders in mind. Using virtual urban simulation increased the transparency, immediacy, direct access, permanence, and follow-up, and it introduced a modern, efficient, and reliable tool for public participation in urban planning.

In another case study, Lopes and Lindstrom (2012) used a virtual city simulation in an urban planning project in the city of Uppsala, Sweden, to evaluate the implementation of a solar-powered Personal Rapid Transit (PRT) system to connect the central train station with several key destination areas in the city. This life-like virtual environment was built using GIS-generated terrain data, buildings that were modeled from actual building facades, a traffic simulation function that was capable of driving thousands of vehicles throughout the virtual area, and dozens of bots that were standing, sitting, or walking to represent pedestrians. The fully interactive model was designed to illustrate the technical and operational concerns regarding the design and locations of the tracks and the stations for the PRT that were to be built in the city. The realistic simulation of structural (buildings, roads, etc.) and dynamic (traffic, pedestrians) elements in an interactive and accessible platform led to high stakeholder involvement. Indeed, the technology played an instrumental part in the decision of stakeholders to promote local efforts and to gather political support at the national level to build the PRT system in Uppsala.

Virtual Reality and City Services

In addition to their wide use in the planning and building fields, both virtual- and augmented-reality technologies are currently used in other services found in cities, from education (i.e., learning and teaching) and training projects to tourism and cultural activities. In fact, the use of these technologies in the current and future services offered by cities is only expected to increase with time as they begin to be applied in new areas. Not only can these technologies be used to increase the level of value in the DIKIW pyramid (Ackoff 1989), but also to increase the exposure of the services that are available as well as the participation of customers in value cocreation.

Visualization (i.e., representing data in a visual context, such as in the form of a chart or a map) is a powerful tool to increase the value of a service and the involvement of all stakeholders in the cocreation and provision of the value (Gawain 2016). In the spirit of the well-known idiom "A picture is worth a thousand words" (i.e., an image can simply present a complex idea), visualization methods are today widely used to illustrate data, information, and sometimes also knowledge in simple schemes. The utility and effectiveness of basic visualization techniques can be markedly increased by combining them with virtual-world technologies that will confer on them 3D and interactive features. For example, rather than representing wind velocity on a static geographical map by simply labeling the map with the forecasted number value of the daily wind speed, wind conditions can be represented using interactive and dynamic wind data that depict its movement on the map. Already used in many fields such as teaching, advertising, art, and more, such techniques can also be used in municipal services.

Among the services that exploit virtual-world technologies and that are already offered by municipalities are location-based services (i.e., mainly GPS-based services that connect service provision with location), which can be used by residents and visitors alike to locate nearby points of interest, such as shops and other businesses and bus stations (Rao and Minakakis 2003; Schiller and Voisard 2004). Indeed, services based on GPS are widely used in cities today to "market" what they have to offer, and interaction with these systems can be initiated either by the customer who searches for information or by the providers (i.e., the municipality and city businesses), who post information for their customers. To add further value to such services, they can be supplemented with augmented-reality technology, which can be used to add virtual noise and pictures to the service (Reitmayr and Schmalstieg 2003; Aurelia, Raj, and Saleh 2014).

VR techniques can also be used to enhance services with experience features—for instance, one that allows customers to "feel" the atmosphere of different businesses, from restaurants to spas, and that provides also tools to enable customers to rate the business and indicate whether they would recommend it to other potential customers. Based on their impression after interaction with that business, the ratings provided by customers will aid in the decision-making processes not only of future customers, whose decision of whether to use the business may be affected by the ratings of previous customers, but also of the provider, for whom the same ratings can indicate areas of the business that should be improved. Another example of the enhancement of services with experience features comprises the sound-and-light shows frequently used today at many tourist sites to present images depicting the history of the place, which could be improved and made more realistic by using augmented-reality technology to add virtual characters to the show.

Virtual Service Characteristics

A prominent part of modern life, the virtual world challenges the traditional definitions and characterizations of provider, customer, and value. Today, the provider usually initiates the process and provides the platform for the technology, even though customers typically use their own devices (e.g., smartphone, dedicated glasses) to operate the system. Customer-initiated VR services, however, have immense untapped potential. A trivial example is a system that allows customers to adjust the ambient atmosphere according to their preferences to optimize their dining time or their sleep. In addition, virtual-reality technology can also be the generator of service in a scenario in which the technology is not merely supplying a different experience during the provision of a value; in addition, the experience itself is also a value. For instance, imagine a virtual service that allows people to purchase virtual cloth by entering a virtual shop, where they can touch, search, choose, and even fit items, and then pay for those items with virtual money. In addition, VR can be used as a substitute for real-life experiences to promote the development of empathy and altruism among people, who may then adopt more sustainably aware behavior. For instance, as most people do not have the opportunity to experience climate change on a daily basis or to feel the concept of biodiversity, VR can introduce everyone to these phenomena, and not just from a cognitive perspective, but also from sensory and behavior points of view. Indeed, by immersing people in unique experiences and allowing them to become active participants rather than mere spectators, VR can influence the public at large. Likewise, VR methods can also contribute to the desired transformation in the service economy of consumers to customers, a shift that is facilitated by increasing their awareness about the effects of consumer behavior. For example, VR can be used to expose consumers to the different stages in a supply chain of a good, from its production in a factory to its acquisition by a consumer in a store to its eventual end of life. The education gained by consumers in this scenario, through their exposure to the entire life cycle of a good, will make them more aware and promote the shift from consumer to customer. Going forward, this scenario also provides the customer with the channel through which to become a provider.

CHAPTER 8

What Next?

Although cities today occupy only 2 percent of the world's land, they are home to 55 percent of the world's population, they account for more than 70 percent of the world's economic activity, they consume 75 percent of natural resources and 85 percent of global energy, and they produce 50 percent of total global waste and about 70 percent of the world's total greenhouse gas emissions (UNEP 2009; UN Habitat 2012). Most existing cities are forecasted to expand in area and population size in the near future when, in addition, many new cities will also be built. These and other changes will alter the city's defining characteristics, from the utilization of natural resources to the construction and operation of physical infrastructures to the systems of administration and provision of services. Likewise, technological advances with the potential to generate new opportunities and promote alternative ways of performing daily tasks will tremendously influence people's way of life.

Insofar as these phenomena will affect urban reality, novel design schemes, in which city livability is allotted top priority, are needed for urban areas and municipal services. Such schemes have the potential to yield resilient cities and vibrant communities by intelligently coordinating the city design process in terms of the city's resources, infrastructure, and administrative needs. The extent to which these novel ideas will have the desired outcome, however, will depend in part on whether the city's various stakeholders use resources, technologies, and services not only for their own benefit, but also for the sake of the greater good of the community. Moreover, because goods ownership and technology should be exploited as tools for achieving resilient communities rather than as targets that people strive to attain (as in the goods-dominant logic), social values will have to be the driving force behind city development and management efforts, including everything from the strategies devised during planning to the actions taken to realize a particular city planning goal.

From the perspective of sustainability, the main question becomes, will the cities of the future be ecocentric (i.e., an ethical stance that defines ecological issues as the top priority in all decisions) or anthropocentric (i.e., an ethical standpoint that views humans as the central or most important element in the universe)?

The United Nations Conference in 2016 on Housing and Sustainable Urban Development (Habitat III) that took place in Quito, Ecuador, proposed a new urban agenda (United Nations 2016). In it the United Nations presented its shared vision of cities of the future, according to which "all inhabitants without discrimination of any kind are able to inhabit and produce just, safe, healthy, accessible, affordable, resilient, and sustainable cities." Also included in that vision are equal rights and opportunities, adequate housing, equal access of all people to public goods, civic participation and engagement, gender equality, accessible urban mobility, disaster management and resilience, environmental sustainability, and high productivity, competitiveness, and innovation by promoting full and productive employment and decent work for all. To address these challenges, new models and paradigms of city design, development, and management were recently proposed.

New Municipal Models

Until not too long ago, cities were allowed to grow more or less spontaneously, almost by accident. Although they were usually logically situated—for example, near an extractable resource, on important trade and transport routes, or in an easily defended area such as a hill or an island—their establishment and growth, unguided and unencumbered by clear notions of urban planning, were seemingly *ex nihilo*.

From its beginnings, urban planning was always bound to utility, and as the field of urban planning matured, added to that utility were the provision of housing, the storage of food and goods, and military defense, which together eventually yielded greater security for city residents. Over time, city design also began to emphasize public convenience, and later, with the advent of the Industrial Revolution, the focus of urban planning was on businesses. As industrial cities were not only centers of production but were also densely populated, they were rife with dangers to human health and safety. These and other drawbacks of the industrial city, in turn, played important roles in driving the shift to modern urban planning paradigms that focus on more people-friendly design, on diversity, and on community livability as higher-priority objectives than business and industrial interests. Lastly, the need to find more efficient ways to use physical and nonphysical resources also yielded new urban planning concepts.

Indeed, the development of urban planning methodologies is an ongoing and dynamic process that must be adapted to two distinctly different types of city development. Besides the anticipated rapid expansion of existing cities in developed countries, more than 80 percent of the cities that will exist in developing countries by 2065 have yet to be built. As such, the principles upon which these unbuilt cities are eventually designed will likely be radically different than, and hopefully improve upon, those that guided the creation of existing cities (Angel 2012).

Regardless of which model(s) a given city uses to guide its development, the city landscape will undoubtedly change in the future as new materials and technologies are realized that will enable city architects to build higher buildings, faster means of transportation, and novel infrastructures. But in addition to identifying new resources that can be used instead of conventional resources to offset the pressure on the latter, people will also have to devise ways to use resources differently. One way that this can be achieved and that has already been successfully applied in several cities is the coupling of urbanism with agriculture by creating gardens, and even entire farms, on the roofs and walls of city buildings. Likewise, issues of resource use in urban planning have been addressed by several new models for city development that have been offered in recent years, among them the models of the compact city (Neuman 2005) and the temporary city (Bishop and Williams 2012).

The compact city envisions settlements with high residential density that practice mixed uses of land and buildings or infrastructures. In so doing, the city promotes not only reductions in resource utilization and in the emission of pollution, it also facilitates the cultivation of an active community life. These goals can be realized first and foremost both by cutting the amounts of infrastructures that need to be built in the city and by using city infrastructures more efficiently. For instance, the compact city is designed to provide fast, accessible, and simple mobility, from walking and cycling to public transportation. It is also founded on assigning varied uses to city areas, such that residential, retail, and commercial interests are combined in the same areas instead of dividing the city space into zones specific to different uses, thus eliminating the need for long-distance journeys to accomplish daily activities (Foord 2010).

Another new municipal development model, the temporary city refers to the opportunistic and ostensibly temporary occupation of vacant and abandoned spaces in existing cities in what has become to be known as the "pop-up" or "meanwhile" phenomenon (Bishop and Williams 2012). These ventures take advantage of the wide variety of dormant municipal spaces (e.g., residential neighborhoods, business districts) plaguing many of today's cities. The visible aftermath of severe downturns in the economic viability of a city, abandoned spaces impose heavy economic and social burdens on cities as long as they remain unused. In the temporary city framework, however, vacant spaces are used for temporary projects and activities, from pop-up shops or stores (i.e., short-time sales spaces) and farmer markets situated along the city's main transportation arteries to temporary housing created from shipping containers. All of these activities effectively repurpose the functions of different city facilities but at a fraction of what those facilities cost their original owners or occupants. Before it was recognized as a viable model for city development, this paradigm was unofficially implemented in various cities beginning in the 1960s, when, to survive in the city, groups of financially constrained artists and activists began squatting illegally in abandoned city areas. Many of today's city planners, architects, and developers, however, now embrace the temporary city as part of a viable new urban model and as an approach that is consistent with the model of sustainability.

Other new municipal models extend beyond the planning and building themes to include, for example, new governance systems. Case in point is the model of the charter city that, adopted by Hong Kong, comprises a city governed by a country other than that within whose borders it exists. The charter city concept can also be applied to a city that chooses to adopt a constitution and system of governance that differ markedly from those of its home country (Frederickson, Curtis, and Logan 2001).

Regardless of which model is used in city planning, cities themselves and the nature of life in cities constantly effect social change that, in turn, influences human behavior at the individual and community levels. Without a doubt, cities of the future will function differently. Though anticipated developments such as office and factory workflow automation will boost productivity, they will also markedly change the labor market, displacing people as certain professions disappear but also creating opportunities for the unemployed as new jobs emerge. Furthermore, from transportation to education, many of the fundamental services of cities will be forever altered, which will necessitate that people change their lifestyles. But will the cities of the future give priority to public good over private interests? The notion of a people-oriented or people-friendly city refers today to an accessible city, where physical but also social mobility is possible for all. At its most basic level, however, the people-friendly concept can be easily adapted to a range of applications in the city realm, from easily accessible municipal services to the right to live in a healthy city.

Finally, another important characteristic of future cites will be the sharing of tangible and intangible values as well as of public and private spaces. These sharing activities are also expected to change the balance between tangible and intangible provision and to create new social values and interactions.

Everything Is Service

The revolutionary service-dominant logic (SDL) paradigm proposed by Vargo and Lush (2004) envisions everything in a given space (e.g., city, community, neighborhood) as essentially a service. In other words, in the service-dominant framework, all tangible and intangible values are created via the production and delivery of services. As such, the exchange of goods and physical resources should be seen as part of the provision of intangible rather than tangible values. Additionally, the SDL dictates that services are jointly created by both the provider and the customer, both of whom are responsible (to varying degrees, depending on the type of service) for the provision of the physical and nonphysical resources needed to cocreate the value. Spohrer et al. (2007) argued that the complexity of services, which include myriad disciplines and stakeholders in the field and whose survival depends on innovation, requires that their study, development, and implementation be organized and systematic (i.e., service science). Extending the notion of value in the frame of sustainable service, Wolfson et al. (2010, 2015) claimed that every service is composed of core-value, or the essence of the service, and super-value, which refers to supported and complementary values. Moreover, their model of sustainable service assigns the roles of provider and customer to either current or future generations and even to technologies or devices. In addition, they claimed that consumers must not only actively participate in the production and delivery of the service, thus transforming into customers, they should also return value to the value pool in their role as providers (Wolfson 2016). In general, therefore, these different frameworks strive to generate more advanced values in a process that encompasses the relevant stakeholders and different subvalues as well as the progression of the value in the value hierarchy, from data to wisdom.

Moving from GDL to SDL (i.e., from solutions that are based on the production and delivery of physical resources and tangible values to those based on the provision of nonphysical resources and intangible values) is by no doubt one of the main changes that human society faces today, and a big step toward sustainability. It requires new perspective and attitude regarding value production and delivery, in which instead of food purchase and consumption, satiety or pleasure will be provided; instead of buying clothing or other fashion items, body covering and protection will be offered; and the purchase of electricity or fuel will be replaced by room temperature supply (i.e., cooling or heating). This initiative not only shifts the focus from physical to nonphysical resources and thus allows more efficient and effective use of natural resources, it also obliges the cocreation of values, thus leading to more responsible provision and to commitment of all stakeholders, direct and indirect. In this respect, the shareconomy that accounts for the sharing of resources, assets, goods, and services and is based on replacement of ownership by access adds intangible values such as knowledge and skills to tangible values to yield more effective and higher-level value. Further, ICTs and virtual-reality technologies will clearly also play an important role in the shift from GDL to SDL. They will open new channels to online, real-time, and long-distance services that make unnecessary the need to spend natural resources to perform tasks and that replace physical resources with nonphysical resources, such as downloading music instead of buying a CD or ordering a flight ticket without going to the travel agency. At last, virtual-reality technologies will also allow ownership and materialism to be replaced by feelings and experiences—for instance, having a sense of feeling without really touching things, or smelling or tasting food without actually eating.

Services in Future Cities

Though the city itself can be defined in terms of a whole or holistic service, it is in fact a space of services. As such, future city services should be redesigned with respect to the production, delivery, and use of municipal services and the roles played by, as well as the interaction between, all stakeholders. In addition, this redesign process should also account for, and indeed promote, the generation of new services and the need to coordinate and match different city services in terms of their logistics, target population segment, and value.

The anticipated, unavoidable growth in the number and sizes of cities in the near future will likely magnify the problems and challenges that they will face. Although urbanization and city living engender many benefits, from organizing people's lives and enabling the cultivation of rich social and economic networks to the centralization of services, they also typically augment pollution and poverty. To ameliorate their negative effects, therefore, future cities will have to address a range of challenges, from resource shortages to water and food security to climate change to compliance with new technologies to the acceptance and support of new social orders. Moreover, they will be confronted with new ways of living, from how we work, move, buy, and meet, to how we produce and deliver services such as education and health care. Cities will thus have to be flexible and able to quickly adapt to changes and propose new channels to fulfill their goals. But in this respect, future cities will also have to themselves dictate different ways of living as part of their core- and super-values.

From the perspectives of service and sustainability, the value cocreation process should result in higher value and rely on fewer resources. In pursuit of this goal, city services should focus on five main hubs:

(1) solution-oriented services, (2) wise services, (3) shared services, (4) human-centered services, and (5) sustainable services.

> **Solution-oriented services**—The cities of today provide services mainly according to the value in-exchange model, which is actually better suited to the provision of goods. Though city infrastructures such as roads or traffic lights and utility supplies such as water or electricity focus mainly on the provision of physical resources, they are delivered via services. Even in the case of self-services, which are provided through the value in-use model and which require higher cocreation levels and greater investments of resources, effort, and knowledge by the customer, such as payments for different city services (e.g., municipal rate, parking toll), the design and development of these services are still attributed mainly to city authorities. On the other hand, by altering the conceptualization of city services, the city or any authorized provider within the city can supply a journey rather than transport facilities or temperature instead of fuel and heating or cooling devices (i.e., solution-based instead of problem-based services). Solution-based or result-oriented services focus on solutions rather than on problems, and both the provider and the customer agree on an outcome or a solution and on the respective parts both play in its provision. Solution-based services, therefore, usually require higher levels of cocreation, where the consumer is an active customer who can also become and function as a provider.

> **Wise services**—The bulk of direct municipal services (i.e., services where citizens or other stakeholders connect with the city authorities) are situated in the lower levels of the value hierarchy that supply data or information (Ackoff 1989), such as about garbage collection schedules or the parking options available in the city. Yet the city also produces higher knowledge, intelligence, and wisdom values that today are mainly provided to the customer indirectly. For example, the city's master plan affects all its citizens, regardless of whether they were directly involved in its production and delivery. Enhancing value either by increasing the level of value cocreation with the customer (e.g., resident or business) or by allowing

every stakeholder in the city to be part of the provision will yield smart services in greater numbers. In addition, the application of a broad and future-oriented perspective of services that considers the mutual relations of each with other services as well as the integration of services will also increase their value. Stated simply, the emphasis in the frame of wise services should be on the generation of quality values and not only on the quantity of services.

Shared services—As the shareconomy gains in prominence, increasingly greater numbers of services will be produced and delivered by sharing data, information, and knowledge in open codes. An open-code or open-source model is based on the collaboration of values, where every customer and provider shares the value and nobody owns it. This type of peer production was introduced in the field of software development and use—for example, open-code software such as Blender, a free and open-source 3D creation suite (Blender 2017)—where developers and organizations spread around the globe share code toward their joint aim to develop a program (Lerner and Tirole 2002). Today the same concept is applied in many other fields, from information-sharing platforms such as Wikipedia and the open-source research field in solar energy (Pearce, Babasola, and Andrews 2012) to open-code governance (Citron 2008). Open-source services are those that allow everyone to be a customer and provider and to produce or use the service simultaneously. A highly successful example of an open-source service is Waze, the largest community-based traffic and navigation application today. In the city arena, shared services will not only be generated top-down, from the municipality to the citizens, they will also be created in bottom-up fashion, from the citizen to the city authorities, or produced and delivered by different stakeholders in the city in an open system.

Human-centered services—User-centered design seeks to foresee how users are likely to use a product in terms of goods or services. Human-centered design refers to a more precise, tailor-made design to suit the specific needs and skills of the person for whom it was designed rather than aiming to fulfill the general needs of "the average person." This design paradigm strives to integrate the social and cognitive sciences with technology (Cooley 2000). So-called socio-technical design models are implemented in many sectors, from community design and architectural design to industrial design, and they aim to increase the efficiency and productivity of the product while improving the user's experience. In addition, a socio-technical approach is exploited in efforts invested in the integration of computing systems and human activities (i.e., human-centered computing) (Jaimes, Sebe, and Gatica-Perez 2006). Recently, Maglio, Kwan, and Spohrer (2015) argued that because service necessarily involves coordinated action among people and technologies, human-centered services yield higher value and thus better service. Another type of human-centered services is personalized services, which are more specialized services that target customer preferences rather than just customer needs. Personalized services, therefore, focus on wants (and not just on needs) and on habits and culture, which are not easy to change, rather than on the creation of higher value. As such, personalized services are not necessarily more effective or more efficient.

Sustainable services—To successfully confront the huge challenges forecasted for future cities, every service that is produced and delivered in the city, either by the authorities or by citizens, businesses, or tourists, must be imbued with sustainability. One step toward the achievement of this goal is adopting the notion of circular services, which are based both on the rational use of physical and nonphysical resources in each value provision and on the integration and synchronization of different services that will eventually be performed in concert. Finally, to truly yield higher value, sustainable services also require that social and environmental values and technologies be matched more efficiently.

Role of Education

Education is a central means with which to equip people with knowledge, ways of thinking and behaving, and confidence not only to fortify their lives, but also to support and implement change in the community and in society as a whole. As such, the education system is one of the main routes to combine theory with action, making it a principal driver of innovation and entrepreneurship. Thus, higher education programs in the fields of service, sustainability, and sustainable services, in general, and those that focus on sustainable municipal services in particular, should be delivered with the goal of supporting the required and anticipated societal shift from GDL to SDL in future city services. However, current education systems, from schools to universities, are run using outdated principles and methods, and therefore they cannot cope with the many technological, social, and cultural changes undergone by human society in just the last half century. In efforts to address the shortcomings of current education systems, therefore, alternative education and learning systems based on novel ideas, from pedagogical approaches to learning environments, are currently under experimental investigation.

If we consider the goal of imbuing everything that the city has to offer with sustainability, education, in the broad sense of the word, has a crucial part to play. The major changes required in our ways of thinking and behavior to realize sustainable development cannot be achieved with technological means, political regulations, or financial instruments alone. As was already noted by the proposition of Agenda 21 [(i.e., the United Nations action plan for sustainable development offered at the Earth Summit held in June 1992 in Rio de Janeiro, Brazil (United Nations 1992)], education is an essential tool for achieving sustainable development. In that task, education needs to combine knowledge, skills, and values to address the environmental and social challenges of the coming decades. UNESCO stated that education for sustainable development should be based on integrating key sustainable development issues into teaching and learning. This may include, for example, instruction about climate change, disaster risk reduction, biodiversity, and poverty reduction and sustainable consumption. It also requires participatory teaching and learning methods that motivate and empower learners to change their behaviors and take action for sustainable development. Education for sustainable development consequently promotes competencies like critical thinking, imagining future scenarios and making decisions in a collaborative way (UNESCO 2013).

In addition, education should also offer revolutionary perspectives about our way of living and our place in the world. This also applies to the city's activities and conduct, where education should affect sustainability in four major areas: (1) philosophy—moving from an anthropocentric or egocentric to an ecocentric perspective and from the attainment of personal benefits to the realization of better quality of life for everybody; (2) implementation—provide the tools and methods needed to practically apply sustainability theory and implement it in daily life; (3) decision making—strive for more efficient and effective decisions at the individual, municipal, and community levels; and (4) quality of life—improve the social, economic, and environmental well-being of all stakeholders.

Although service-sector activities have constituted an important subject of research for many years, most of it was focused on marketing or management in terms of the economic aspects of services. Yet as the service sector is much broader and multidisciplinary, it should be defined as a science (i.e., service science) whose study involves the integration of numerous disciplines, such as economics, marketing, computer science, and the cognitive sciences in a format similar to that offered by IBM (IBM Almaden Services Research 2006; Spohrer et al. 2007; Maglio and Spohrer 2007; Maglio, Kieliszewski, and Spohrer 2010). Though a relative newcomer in the academic world, this scientific discipline is offered by several universities that have programs in service science or in the widespread service science, management, and engineering. Graduates of these programs are already working in a variety of industries, from computer companies to firms that specialize in the provision of services—for example, law and insurance firms. Indeed, with the increased awareness of the importance and complexity of service systems and networks and in light of the prominent place that SDL is expected to occupy in future markets and societies as well as in city operations, service philosophers, scientists, and engineers and other service experts will fulfill important roles in the design, development, and management of processes.

References

Ackoff, R.L. 1989. "From Data to Wisdom." *Journal of Applied Systems Analysis* 16, no. 1, pp. 3–9.

Aitken, R., D. Ballantyne, P. Osborne, and J. Williams. 2006. "Introduction to the Special Issue on the Service-Dominant Logic of Marketing: Insights from The Otago Forum." pp. 275–80.

Aldaya, M.M., A.K. Chapagain, A.Y. Hoekstra, and M.M Mekonnen. 2012. *The Water Footprint Assessment Manual: Setting the Global Standard.* Oxford: Routledge.

Allee, A. 2008. "Value Network Analysis and Value Conversion of Tangible and Intangible Assets." *Journal of Intellectual Capital* 9, no. 1, pp. 5–24.

Alshehri, M., and S. Drew. 2010. "E-Government Fundamentals." IADIS International Conference ICT, Society and Human Beings.

American Public Transportation Association. 2015. *2015 Public Transportation Fact Book.* Washington, DC.

Andreassen, T.W. 1994. "Satisfaction, Loyalty and Reputation as Indicators of Customer Orientation in the Public Sector." *International Journal of Public Sector Management* 7, no. 2, pp. 16–34.

Andersen, M.S. 2007. "An Introductory Note on the Environmental Economics of the Circular Economy." *Sustainability Science* 2, no. 1, pp. 133–40.

Anderson, P.L., M. Price, S.M. Edwards, M.A. Obasaju, S.K. Schmertz, E. Zimand, and M.R. Calamaras. 2013. "Virtual Reality Exposure Therapy for Social Anxiety Disorder: A Randomized Controlled Trial." *Journal of Consulting and Clinical Psychology* 81, no. 5, pp. 751–60.

Angel, S. 2012. *Planet of Cities.* Cambridge, MA: Lincoln Institute of Land Policy.

Ashton, J. 1991. *Healthy Cities.* Milton Keynes: Open University Press.

Aurelia, S., M.D. Raj, and O. Saleh. 2014. "Mobile Augmented Reality and Location Based Service." *Advances in Information Science and Applications* 2, pp. 551–58.

Barker, G. 2009. *The Agricultural Revolution in Prehistory: Why Did Foragers Become Farmers?* Oxford: Oxford University Press.

Batty, M., K.W. Axhausen, F. Giannotti, A. Pozdnoukhov, A. Bazzani, M. Wachowicz, and Y. Portugali. 2012. "Smart Cities of the Future." *The European Physical Journal Special Topics* 214, no. 1, pp. 481–518.

Benington, J. 1986. "Local Economic Strategies: Paradigms for a Planned Economy?" *Local Economy* 1, no. 1, pp. 7–24.

Biljecki, F., J. Stoter, H. Ledoux, S. Zlatanova, and A. Çöltekin. 2015. "Applications of 3D City Models: State of the Art Review." *ISPRS International Journal of Geo-Information* 4, no. 4, pp. 2842–89.

Billinghurst, M., A. Clark, and G. Lee. 2015. "A Survey of Augmented Reality." *Foundations and Trends® Human–Computer Interaction* 8, nos. 2–3, pp. 73–272.

Biocca, F., and M.R. Levy. 2013. *Communication in the Age of Virtual Reality.* Oxford: Routledge.

Bishop, P., and L. Williams. 2012. *The Temporary City.* London: Routledge.

Blender 2.79. https://blender.org/

Bluestone, D.M. 1988. "Detroit's City Beautiful and the Problem of Commerce." *Journal of the Society of Architectural Historians* XLVII, no. 3, pp. 245–62.

Brown, A., and T. Green. 2016. "Virtual Reality: Low-Cost Tools and Resources for the Classroom." *TechTrends* 60, no. 5, pp. 517–19.

Brundtland, G.H. 1987. "Our Common Future." World Commission for Environment and Development.

Bryson, J.S. 2002. *Ecopoetry: A Critical Introduction.* Salt Lake: University of Utah Press.

Buder, S. 1990. *Visionaries and Planners: The Garden City Movement and the Modern Community.* Oxford: Oxford University Press.

Bury, J.B. 1987. *The Idea of Progress: An Inquiry into its Origin and Growth.* Courier Corporation.

Campbell, C.S., P.P. Maglio, and M. Davis, 2011. "From Self-Service to Super-Service: How to Shift the Boundary Between Customer and Provider." *Information System and E-Business Management* 9, pp. 173–91.

Caragliu, A., C. Del Bo, and P. Nijkamp. 2011. "Smart Cities in Europe." *Journal of Urban Technology* 18, no. 2, pp. 65–82.

Chandler, T.1987. *Four Thousand Years of Urban Growth: An Historical Census.* Lampeter: The Edwin Mellen Press.

Chandler, J.D., and S.L. Vargo. 2011. "Contextualization and Value-in-Context: How Context Frames Exchange." *Marketing Theory* 11, no. 1, pp. 5–49.

Cheng, M. 2016. "Sharing Economy: A Review and Agenda for Future Research." *International Journal of Hospitality Management* 57, pp. 60–70.

Chester, M.V., and H. Arpad. 2009. "Environmental Assessment of Passenger Transportation Should Include Infrastructure and Supply Chains." *Environmental Research Letter* 4, no. 2, pp. 1–8.

Childe, V.G. 1936. *Man Makes Himself.* London: Watts and Co.

Childe, V.G. 1950. "The Urban Revolution." *The Town Planning Review* 21, no. 1, pp. 3–17.

Citron, D.K. 2008. "Open Code Governance." The University of Chicago Legal Forum.

City of Dallas. 2016. Report A16-006. http://tinyurl.com/m6493d6

City of Novato, CA. 2013. The National Citizen Survey.

Citypopulation.de. Retrieved. 2010. Principal Agglomerations of the World.

Coeterier, J.F. 1994. "Liveliness in Town Centers." In *The Urban Experience - A People-Environment Perspective* (Proceedings 13th International Conference of the IAPS), eds. S.J. Neary, M.S. Symes, and F.E. Brown, 297–311.

Cooley, M. 2000. "Human-Centered Design." In *Information Design,* ed. R. Jacobson, 59–81. Cambridge: MIT Press.

Crespo, A.B., G.G. Idrovo, N. Rodrigues, and A. Pereira. 2016. "A Virtual Reality UAV Simulation with Body Area Networks to Promote the Elders Life Quality. In Technology and Innovation in Sports, Health and Wellbeing TISHW." International Conference on IEEE. pp. 1–7.

Davies, Z.G., J.L. Edmondson, A. Heinemeyer, J.R. Leake, and K.J. Gaston. 2011. "Mapping an Urban Ecosystem Service: Quantifying Above-Ground Carbon Storage at a City-Wide Scale." *Journal of Applied Ecology* 48, no. 5, pp. 1125–34.

Day, G.S. 1981. "The Product Life Cycle: Analysis and Applications Issues." *The Journal of Marketing* 45, no. 4, pp. 60–67.

Demirkan, H., J.C. Spohrer, and V. Krishna. 2011. "Service and Science." In *The Science of Service Systems,* eds. H. Demirkan, J.C. Spohrer, and V. Krishna, 325–58. New York: Springer.

Dresner, S. 2008. *The Principles of Sustainability.* Oxford: EarthScan.

Earnshaw, R.A. 2014. *Virtual Reality Systems.* Cambridge: Academic Press.

Emery, I., and S. Brown. 2016. "Lettuce to Reduce Greenhouse Gases: A Comparative Life Cycle Assessment of Conventional and Community Agriculture." In *Sowing Seeds in the City,* 161–69. Amsterdam: Springer.

Homberger, E., and A. Hudson. 2005. *The Historical Atlas of New York City.* Oxford: Owl Books.

Etezadzadeh, C. 2015. *Smart City–Future City?: Smart City 2.0 as a Livable City and Future Market.* Heidelberg: Springer.

European Union. 2011. *Cities of Tomorrow: Challenges, Visions, Ways Forward.*

European Commission. 2014. *Wasted Potential! Towards Circular Economy in Cities.* 16th European Forum on Eco-Innovation.

Finkbeiner, M., E.M. Schau, A. Lehmann, and M. Traverso. 2010. "Towards Life Cycle Sustainability Assessment." *Sustainability* 2, no. 10, pp. 3309–22.

Finnveden, G., M.Z. Hauschild, T. Ekvall, J. Guinée, R. Heijungs, S. Hellweg, and S. Suh. 2009. "Recent Developments in Life Cycle Assessment." *Journal of Environmental Management* 91, no. 1, pp. 1–21.

Flint, J., and M. Raco. 2012. *The Future of Sustainable Cities: Critical Reflections.* Bristol: Policy Press.

Frederickson, H.G., C. Wood, and B. Logan. 2001. "How American City Governments have Changed: The Evolution of the Model City Charter." *National Civic Review* 90, no. 1, pp. 3–18.

Frug, G.E. 1998. "City Services." *New York University Law Rev.*, 73, pp. 23–96.

Foord, J. 2010. "Mixed-Use Trade-Offs: How to Live and Work in a Compact City Neighbourhood." *Built Environment* 36, no. 1, pp. 47–62.

Gautam, P. 2011. "Social Life Cycle Assessment of Solid Waste Management in Kathmandu City Nepal." Proceedings of the Life Cycle Management 2011 Conference, Berlin.

Gawain, S. 2016. *Creative Visualization: Use the Power of Your Imagination to Create What You Want in Your Life*. Novato: New World Library.

Ghisellini, P., C. Cialani, and S. Ulgiati. 2016. "A Review on Circular Economy: The Expected Transition to a Balanced Interplay of Environmental and Economic Systems." *Journal of Cleaner Production* 114, pp. 11–32.

Gibson, C. 2007. Population of the 100 Largest Cities and Other Urban Places in the United States: 1790 to 1990. United States Census Bureau, June 1998.

Girardet, H. 2017. "Regenerative Cities." In *Green Economy Reader*, ed. S. Shmelev, 183–204. Heidelberg: Springer.

Glazebrook, G. 2009. "Taking the Con Out of Convenience: The True Cost of Transport Modes in Sydney." *Urban Policy and Research* 27, no. 1, pp. 5–24.

Google Environmental Report. 2017. https://environment.google/ (accessed February 26, 2017).

Gretchen, C.D. 1997. *Nature's Services, Societal Dependence on Natural Ecosystems*. Washington, DC: Island Press.

Hall, A.C. 1996. *Design Control; Towards a New Approach*. Oxford: Butterworth Architecture.

Hartanto, D., I.L. Kampmann, N. Morina, P.G. Emmelkamp, M.A. Neerincx, and W.P. Brinkman. 2014. "Controlling Social Stress in Virtual Reality Environments." *PloS One* 9, no. 3, p. e92804.

Heinrichs, H. 2013. "Sharing Economy: A Potential New Pathway to Sustainability." *Gaia: Ecological Perspectives for Science & Society* 22, no. 4, pp. 228–31.

Henriques, A., and J. Richardson. 2013. *The Triple Bottom Line: Does it All Add Up*. Abingdon: Routledge.

Hitge, G., and M. Vanderschuren. 2015. "Comparison of Travel Time Between Private Car and Public Transport in Cape Town." *Journal of South African Institution of Civil Engineering* 57, no. 3, pp. 35–43.

IBM Almaden Services Research. 2006. *Service Science, Management, and Engineering (SSME): Challenges, Frameworks, and Call for Participation*. San Jose: IBM Almaden Research Center.

Information Resources Management Association. 2014. Open Source Technology: Concepts, Methodologies, Tools, and Applications. IGI Global.

International Organization for Standardization, ISO 37120. 2014.

Isaac, E., and S. Brown. 2016. "Lettuce to Reduce Greenhouse Gases: A Comparative Life Cycle Assessment of Conventional and Community Agriculture." In *Sowing Seeds in the City*, eds. S. Brown, K. McIvor, and E.H. Snyder, 161–69. Heidelberg: Springer.

Jabareen, Y. 2013. "Planning the Resilient City: Concepts and Strategies for Coping with Climate Change and Environmental Risk." *Cities* 31, pp. 220–29.

Jackson, K. 1995. *Encyclopedia of New York City*. New Haven: Yale University Press.

Jaimes, A., N. Sebe, and D. Gatica-Perez. 2006. "Human-Centered Computing: A Multimedia Perspective." Proceedings of the 14th ACM International Conference on Multimedia. ACM.

Jenks, M., and C. Jones. 2009. *Dimensions of the Sustainable City*, Vol. 2. Springer Science & Business Media.

Joassart-Marcelli, P., and J. Musso. 2005. "Municipal Service Provision Choices Within a Metropolitan Area." *Urban Affairs Review* 40, no. 4, pp. 492–519.

Jørgensen, A., A. Le Bocq, L. Nazarkina, and M. Hauschild. 2008. "Methodologies for Social Life Cycle Assessment." *The International Journal of Life Cycle Assessment* 13, no. 2, pp. 96–103.

Johnston R., and P. Jones. 2004. "Service Productivity: Towards Understanding the Relationship Between Operational and Customer Productivity." *International Journal of Productivity and Performance Management* 53, no. 3, pp. 201–13.

Jolliet, O., M. Saadé-Sbeih, S. Shaked, A. Jolliet, and P. Crettaz. 2015. *Environmental Life Cycle Assessment*. Boca Raton: CRC Press.

Kalawsky, R. 1993. *The Science of Virtual Reality and Virtual Environments: A Technical, Scientific and Engineering Reference on Virtual Environments*. Wokingham: Addison-Wesley.

Kantorová, K., and T. Růžička. 2015. "Measuring Citizen Satisfaction: Prospects for Using a Questionnaire to Manage Relationships Between Local Governments and Citizens in the Czech Republic." *Acta Academica Karviniensia* 15, no. 3, pp. 30–42.

Kelly, J.M., and D. Swindell. 2002. "A Multiple–Indicator Approach to Municipal Service Evaluation: Correlating Performance Measurement and Citizen Satisfaction Across Jurisdictions." *Public Administration Review* 62, no. 5, pp. 610–21.

Kennedy, C., S. Pincetl, and P. Bunje. 2011. "The Study of Urban Metabolism and its Applications to Urban Planning and Design." *Environmental Pollution* 159, no. 8, pp. 1965–73.

Kenneth, T.J. 1995. *The Encyclopedia of New York City*. New Haven: Yale University Press.

Kenworthy, J., and F. Laube. 2001. "The Millennium Cities Database for Sustainable Transport." International Association of Public Transport, Belgium.

Khodabakhsh, P., H. Fathi, and S. Mashayekhi. 2016. "Planning for Future Urban Services in the Smart City Era: Integrating e-services in Urban Planning Process." *Armanshahr Architecture & Urban Development* 9, no. 16, pp. 153–68.

Kiesler, S. 2014. *Culture of the Internet.* Hove: Psychology Press.

Kirchner, J.W. 2002. "The Gaia Hypothesis: Fact, Theory, and Wishful Thinking." *Climatic Change* 52, no. 4, pp. 391–408.

Kitzes, J. 2013. "An Introduction to Environmentally-Extended Input-Output Analysis." *Resources* 2, pp. 489–503.

Larice, M., and E. Macdonald. 2013. *The Urban Design Reader.* San Francisco: Routledge.

Lehmann, S. 2010. *The Principles of Green Urbanism: Transforming the City for Sustainability.* Oxford: Earthscan.

Lerner, J., and J. Tirole. 2002. "Some Simple Economics of Open Source." *The Journal of Industrial Economics* 50, no. 2, pp. 197–234.

Li, X., Z. Lv, W. Wang, C. Wu, and J. Hu. 2015. "Virtual Reality Gis and Cloud Service Based Traffic Analysis Platform." In Geoinformatics, 23rd International Conference on Geoinformatics. IEEE, pp. 1–6.

Lin, P.J., C.C. Kao, K.H. Lam, and I.C. Tsai. 2014. "Design and Implementation of a Tourism System Using Mobile Augmented Reality and Gis Technologies." In Proceedings of the 2nd International Conference on Intelligent Technologies and Engineering Systems (ICITES2013), pp. 1093–99. Springer International Publishing.

Lin, S., H.F. Cheng, W. Li, Z.W. Huang, P. Hui, and C. Peylo. 2017. "Ubii: Physical World Interaction Through Augmented Reality." *IEEE Transactions on Mobile Computing* 16, no. 3, pp. 872–85.

Litman, T. 2015. "Evaluating Public Transit Benefits and Costs." Victoria Transport Policy Institute.

Litman, T. 2007. "Developing Indicators for Comprehensive and Sustainable Transport Planning." *Transportation Research Record: Journal of the Transportation Research Board* 2017, pp. 10–15.

Loomis, J.M. 2016. "Presence in Virtual Reality and Everyday Life: Immersion Within a World of Representation." *Teleoperators and Virtual Environments* 25, no. 2, pp. 169–74.

Lopes, C.V., and C. Lindstrom. 2012. "Virtual Cities in Urban Planning: The Uppsala Case Study." *Journal of Theoretical Applied Electronic Commerce Research* 7, pp. 88–100.

Lucas, R.E. 2002. *Lectures on Economic Growth.* Massachusetts: Harvard University Press.

Lusch R.F., and S.L. Vargo. 2006. *The Service-Dominant Logic of Marketing: Dialog, Debate, and Directions.* New York: M.E. Sharpe Inc.

Maglio, P.P., and J.C. Spohrer. 2007. *Fundamentals of Service Science.* San Jose: IBM.

Maglio, P.P., C.A. Kieliszewski, and J.C. Spohrer. 2010. *Handbook of Service Science.* New York: Springer.

Maglio, P.P., S.J. Kwan, and J. Spohrer. 2015. "Commentary—Toward a Research Agenda for Human-Centered Service System Innovation." *Service Science* 7, no. 1, pp. 1–10.

Maslow, A.H. 1943. "A Theory of Human Motivation." *Psychological Review* 50, no. 4, pp. 370–96.

Mellars, P.A., and C. Stringer. 1989. *The Human Revolution: Behavioral and Biological Perspectives in the Origins of Modern Humans.* Edinburgh: Edinburgh University Press.

Miguel, R., A.F. Tavares, and J.F. Araújo. 2012. "Municipal Service Delivery: The Role of Transaction Costs in the Choice Between Alternative Governance Mechanisms." *Local Government Studies* 38, no. 5, pp. 615–38.

Muthu, S.S. 2015. *Social Life Cycle Assessment: An Insight.* Singapore: Springer.

Nam, T., and T.A. Pardo. 2011. "Conceptualizing Smart City with Dimensions of Technology, People, and Institutions." Proceedings of the 12th Annual International Digital Government Research Conference: Digital Government Innovation in Challenging Times.

Narayanaswamy, V., J.A. Scott, J.N. Ness, and M. Lochhead. 2003. "Resource Flow and Product Chain Analysis as Practical Tools to Promote Cleaner Production Initiatives." *Journal of Cleaner Production* 11, no. 4, pp. 375–87.

NationMaster. N.d. http://nationmaster.com/country-info/stats/Transport/Road/Motor-vehicles-per-1000-people (accessed February 26, 2017).

Neuman, M. 2005. "The Compact City Fallacy." *Journal of Planning Education and Research* 25, no. 1, pp. 11–26.

Neuman, W.L., and K. Robson. 2012. *Basics of Social Research: Qualitative and Quantitative Approaches.* Toronto, ON: Pearson.

Newman, P., and I. Jennings. 2012. *Cities as Sustainable Ecosystems: Principles and Practices.* Washington, DC: Island Press.

Nguyen, M.T., H.K. Nguyen, K.D. Vo-Lam, X.G. Nguyen, and M.T. Tran. 2016. "Applying Virtual Reality in City Planning." In International Conference on Virtual, Augmented and Mixed Reality, pp. 724–35. Springer International Publishing.

Niinimäki, K. "Eco-Clothing, Consumer Identity and Ideology." *Sustainable Development* 18, no. 3, pp. 150–62.

Ntiro, S. 2000. *Eastern Africa.* Dar-es-Salaam: KPMG.

Odum, E.P., H.T. Odum, and J. Andrews. 1971. *Fundamentals of Ecology,* Vol. 3. Philadelphia: Saunders.

OECD. 2009. *OECD Regions at a Glance 2009*. Paris: OECD Publishing.

Ohta, Y., and H. Tamura. 2014. *Mixed Reality: Merging Real and Virtual Worlds*. Springer Publishing Company.

Ott, M., and L. Freina. 2015. "A Literature Review on Immersive Virtual Reality in Education: State of the Art and Perspectives." Conference Proceedings of eLearning and Software for Education (eLSE), No. 1. Universitatea Nationala de Aparare Carol I.

Palvia, S.C.J., and S.S. Sharma. 2007. "E-government and E-governance: Definitions/Domain Framework and Status Around the World." International Conference on E-governance, pp. 1–12.

Pauli, G.A. 2010. *The Blue Economy: 10 Years, 100 Innovations, 100 Million Jobs*. Taos: Paradigm Publications.

Pearce, J.M., A. Babasola, and R. Andrews. 2012. "Open Solar Photovoltaic Systems Optimization." In VentureWell. Proceedings of Open, the Annual Conference, p. 1. National Collegiate Inventors & Innovators Alliance.

Pedersen, P., H. Palm, C. Ringsted, and L. Konge, 2014. "Virtual-Reality Simulation to Assess Performance in Hip Fracture Surgery." *Acta Orthopaedica* 85, no. 4, pp. 403–07.

Pernick, R., and C. Wilder. 2007. *The Clean Tech Revolution: The Next Big Growth and Investment Opportunity*. New York: HarperCollins Publishers.

Pepper, D. 2002. *Eco-Socialism: From Deep Ecology to Social Justice*. London: Routledge.

Pile, S. 1999. "What Is a City?" *City worlds*, pp. 3–52.

Porter, M.E. 1985. *Competitive Strategy: Creating and Sustaining Superior Performance*. New York: The Free Press.

Portman, M.E., A. Natapov, and D. Fisher-Gewirtzman. 2015. "To Go Where No Man has Gone Before: Virtual Reality in Architecture, Landscape Architecture and Environmental Planning." *Computers, Environment and Urban Systems* 54, pp. 376–84.

Portney, K. 2005. "Civic Engagement and Sustainable Cities in the United States." *Public Administration Review* 65, no. 5, pp. 579–91.

Qian, G., and C. Wang. 2016. "Circular Economy Cities." In *China's Eco-city Construction*, eds. L. Jingyuan and Y. Tongjin, 169–88. Heidelberg: Springer.

Rao, B., and L. Minakakis. 2003. "Evolution of Mobile Location-Based Services." *Communications of the ACM* 46, no. 12, pp. 61–65.

Ratti, C., and M. Claudel. 2016. *The City of Tomorrow: Sensors, Networks, Hackers, and the Future of Urban Life*. New Haven: Yale University Press.

Reilly, J.M. 2012. "Green Growth and the Efficient Use of Natural Resources." *Energy Economics* 34, pp. S85–S93.

Reitmayr, G., and D. Schmalstieg. 2003. "Location Based Applications for Mobile Augmented Reality." Proceedings of the Fourth Australasian User

Interface Conference on User Interfaces 2003-Volume 18. Australian Computer Society, Inc.

Rix, J., S. Haas, and J. Teixeira. 2016. *Virtual Prototyping: Virtual Environments and the Product Design Process.* Heidelberg: Springer.

Rosenwaike, I. 1972. *Population History of New York City,* 8. Syracuse, New York: Syracuse University Press.

Rossel, P., and M. Finger. 2007. "Conceptualizing E-Governance." In Proceedings of the 1st International Conference on Theory and Practice of Electronic Governance, pp. 399–407. ACM.

Rust, R.T., and R.L. Oliver. 1994. *Service Quality: New Directions in Theory and Practice.* Los-Angeles: Sage Publications.

Satterthwaite, D. 1997. "Sustainable Cities or Cities that Contribute to Sustainable Development?" *Urban studies* 34, no. 10, pp. 1667–91.

Schiller, J., and A. Voisard. 2004. *Location-Based Services.* Amsterdam: Elsevier.

Schmiedeknecht, M.H. 2013. "Environmental Sustainability Index." In *Encyclopedia of Corporate Social Responsibility*, eds. O. Samuel, N.C. Idowu, Z. Liangrong, and D.G. Ananda, 1017–24. Heidelberg: Springer.

Seattle Climate Partnership, HomeStreet bank. 2009. A Carbon Footprint Measurement Case Study. http://nbis.org/nbisresources/case_histories/home street_carbon%20footprint_case_study.pdf (accessed February 26, 2017).

Simpson, D.M. 2001. "Virtual Reality and Urban Simulation in Planning: A Literature Review and Topical Bibliography." *Journal Plan Literature* 15, no. 3, pp. 359–76.

Skudder, H., A. Druckman, J. Cole, A. McInnes, I. Brunton-Smith, and G.P. Ansaloni. 2016. "Addressing the Carbon-Crime Blind Spot: A Carbon Footprint Approach." *Journal of Industrial Ecology,* pp. S1–S11.

Spohrer, J., and P.P. Maglio. 2006. "The Emergence of Service Science: Toward Systematic Service Innovations to Accelerate Co-Creation of Value." IBM Almaden Services Research.

Spohrer, J., P.P. Maglio, J. Bailey, and D. Gruhl. 2007. "Steps Toward a Science of Service Systems." *Computer* 40, no. 1, pp. 71–77.

Spohrer, J., S.L. Vargo, N. Caswell, and P.P. Maglio. 2008. "The Service System is the Basic Abstraction of Service Science." In Hawaii International Conference on System Sciences, Proceedings of the 41st Annual. IEEE.

Spohrer, J. 2011. Whole Service. http://service-science.info/archives/1056

Spohrer, J., P. Piciocchi, and C. Bassano. 2012. "Three Frameworks for Service Research: Exploring Multilevel Governance in Nested, Networked Systems." *Service Science* 4, no. 2, pp. 147–60.

Spohrer, J., C. Bassano, P. Piciocchi, and M.A.K. Siddike. 2016. "What Makes a system smart? Wise?" Proceeding of The 7th International Conference on Applied Human Factors and Ergonomics. Florida, USA.

Stahel, W.R. 2014. "The Business Angle of a Circular Economy: Higher Competitiveness, Higher Resource Security and Material Efficiency." *EMF* 15, pp. 1–10.

Stahel, W.R. 2016. "Circular Economy: A New Relationship with Our Goods and Materials Would Save Resources and Energy and Create Local Jobs." *Nature* 531, no. 7595, pp. 435–39.

Statistics Sweden. 2010 (Corrected 2013). Land Used for Transport Infrastructure.

Stauskis, G. 2014. "Development of Methods and Practices of Virtual Reality as a Tool for Participatory Urban Planning: A Case Study of Vilnius City as an Example for Improving Environmental, Social and Energy Sustainability." *Energy, Sustainability and Society* 4, no. 7, pp. 1–13.

Su, B., A. Heshmati, Y. Geng, and X. Yu. 2013. "A Review of the Circular Economy in China: Moving from Rhetoric to Implementation." *Journal of Cleaner Production* 42, pp. 215–27.

Tertius, C. 1987. *Four Thousand Years of Urban Growth: An Historical Census*. Lewiston: St. David's University Press.

Thorsteinsson, G. 2013. "Developing an Understanding of the Pedagogy of Using a Virtual Reality Learning Environment (VRLE) to Support Innovation Education." In *The Routledge International Handbook of Innovation Education*, ed. L.V. Shavinina, 456–70. Oxford: Routledge.

Townsend, A.M. 2013. *Smart Cities: Big Data, Civic Hackers, and the Quest for a New Utopia*. WW Norton & Company.

United Nation. 1992. Agenda 21. https://sustainabledevelopment.un.org/content/documents/Agenda21.pdf

UN Habitat. 2012. Hot Cities: Battle-Ground for Climate Change. http://mirror.unhabitat.org/downloads/docs/E_Hot_Cities.pdf

United Nations Conference on Housing and Sustainable Urban Development (Habitat III). 2016. https://habitat3.org/bitcache/99d99fbd0824de50214e99f864459d 8081a9be00?vid=591155&disposition=inline&op=view

UNESCO. 2013. Education for Sustainable Development (ESD). Paris, UNESCO. http://unesco.org/new/en/education/themes/leading-the-international-agenda/education-for- sustainable-development

UNEP Shifting to Resource Efficient Cities: 8 Key Messages for Policy Makers. http://unep.org/resourceefficiency/Portals/24147/scp/REC/1307-GIREC-A4-HD.pdf

United States Census Bureau. 2016. *Annual Estimates of the Resident Population. April 1, 2010 to July 1, 2015, 2015 Population Estimates*. New York.

US Green Building Council. 2009. "LEED for Neighborhood Development." A Prescription for Green Healthy Communities.

Vargo, S.L., and R.F. Lusch. 2004. "Evolving to a New Dominant Logic for Marketing." *Journal of Marketing* 68, pp. 1–17.

Vargo, S.L., P.P. Maglio, and M.A. Akaka. 2008. "On Value and Value Co-Creation: A Service Systems and Service Logic Perspective." *European Management Journal* 26, no. 3, pp. 145–52.

Vivier, J. 2006. "Mobility in Cities Database: Better Mobility for People Worldwide." International Association of Public Transport, Belgium.

Wackernagel, M., and W. Rees. 1998. *Our Ecological Footprint: Reducing Human Impact on the Earth (No. 9)*. Gabriola Island: New Society Publishers.

Weidema, B.P., M. Thrane, P. Christensen, J. Schmidt, and S. Løkke. 2008. "Carbon Footprint." *Journal of industrial Ecology* 12, no. 1, pp. 3–6.

Weisel, A. 2015. "Virtual Reality and the Psyche: Some Psychoanalytic Approaches to Media Addiction." *Journal of Analytical Psychology* 60, no. 2, pp. 198–219.

Wiedmann, T., and J. Barrett. 2011. "A Greenhouse Gas Footprint Analysis of UK Central Government, 1990–2008." *Environmental Science and Policy* 14, no. 8, pp. 1041–51.

Wright, H., and S.E. Hollingshead. 2011. "Effect of Localizing Fruit and Vegetable Consumption on Greenhouse Gas Emissions and Nutrition, Santa Barbara County." *Environmental Science & Technology* 45, no. 10, pp. 4555–62.

Wolfson, A., D. Tavor, and S. Mark, M. Schermann, and H. Krcmar. 2010. "S³-Sustainability and Services Science: Novel Perspective and Challenge." *Service Science* 2, no. 4, pp. 216–24.

Wolfson, A., D. Tavor, and S. Mark. 2011. "Sustainable Services: The Natural Mimicry Approach." *Journal of Service Science and Management* 4, no. 2, pp. 125–31.

Wolfson A., D. Tavor, and S. Mark. 2012. "Sustainability and Shifting from a 'Person to Person' to a Super- or Self-service." *International Journal of u- and e- Service, Science and Technology* 5, no. 1, pp. 25–34.

Wolfson, A., D. Tavor, and S. Mark. 2013. "Editorial Column—From CleanTech to CleanServ." *Service Science* 5, no. 3, pp. 193–96.

Wolfson, A., D. Tavor, and S. Mark. 2014. "CleanServs: Clean Services for a More Sustainable World." *Sustainability Accounting, Management and Policy Journal* 5, no. 4, pp. 405–24.

Wolfson, A., S. Mark, P.M. Martin, and D. Tavor. 2015. *Sustainability through Service: Perspectives, Concepts and Examples*. Heidelberg: Springer.

Wolfson, A. 2016. *Sustainable Service*. New-York: Business Expert Publisher.

World Commission on Environment and Development. 1987. *Our Common Future*. Oxford: Oxford University Press.

The World Population Prospects. 2015. *Population Division, World Urbanization Prospects: The 2015 Revision*. United Nations Publications.

Wu, R., D. Yang, and J. Chen. 2014. "Social Life Cycle Assessment Revisited." *Sustainability* 6, no. 7, pp. 4200–26.

Yang, Y., and J.E. Campbell. 2017. "Improving Attributional Life Cycle Assessment for Decision Support: The Case of Local Food in Sustainable Design." *Journal of Cleaner Production* 145, pp. 361–66.

Youniss, J., J.A. Mclellan, Y. Su, and M. Yates. 1999. "The Role of Community Service in Identity Development Normative, Unconventional, and Deviant Orientations." *Journal of Adolescent Research* 14, no. 2, pp. 248–61.

Zang, S., C. Wu, H. Liu, and X. Na. 2011. "Impact of Urbanization on Natural Ecosystem Service Values: A Comparative Study." *Environmental Monitoring and Assessment* 179, nos. 1–4, pp. 575–88.

Zhang, S., and A.B. Moore. 2014. "The Usability of Online Geographic Virtual Reality for Urban Planning." In *Innovations in 3D Geo-Information Sciences*, ed. U. Isikdag, 225–42. Springer International Publishing.

Index

www.ingramcontent.com/pod-product-compliance
Lightning Source LLC
Chambersburg PA
CBHW071905200326

41519CB00016B/4510